California

CALIFORNIA BY ROAD

Celebrate the States

California

Linda Jacobs Altman

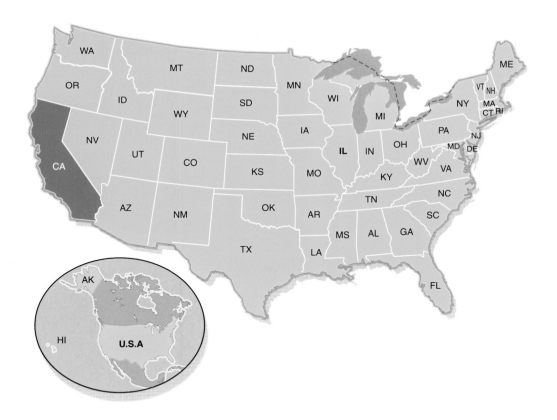

Marshall Cavendish
Benchmark
New York

Marshall Cavendish Benchmark
99 White Plains Road
Tarrytown, New York 10591-9001
www.marshallcavendish.us

All Internet sites were correct and accurate when sent to press.

Library of Congress Cataloging-in-Publication Data

Altman, Linda Jacobs, 1943–
California / by Linda Jacobs Altman.
p. cm. — (Celebrate the states)
Summary: "An exploration of the geography, history, economy, people,
government, and landmarks of California"—Provided by publisher.
Includes bibliographical references and index.
ISBN 0-7614-1737-0
1. California—Juvenile literature. I. Title. II. Series.
F861.3.A45 2005   979.4—dc22   2005006456

Photo research by Candlepants Incorporated

Cover photo: Carmel Studios/SuperStock

The photographs in this book are used by permission and through the courtesy of: *Photo Researchers Inc.*: Adam Jones, 8, 16, back cover; Tom McHugh, 23; Spencer Grant, 55; David R. Frazier, 76; Lawrence Migdale, 77, 121. *Corbis:* Galen Rowell, 11; Darrell Gullin, 21; 30; Bettmann, 35, 36, 39, 40, 128, 131; Roger Ressmeyer, 43, 102; Charles O'Rear, 44, 83, 104; Richard Cummins, 66, 97; Orjan F. Ellingvag, 70; Kim Kulish, 71, 90; Henry Diltz, 72; Ted Soqui, 74; Reuters, 85; Lester Lefkowitz, 88; Bruce Burkhardt, 92; John & Lisa Merrill, 95; Joseph Sohm/ChromoSohm Inc. 101; Phil Schermeister, 107; Eric & David Hosking, 111; Thom Lang, 120; Sygma, 125; Hulton-Deutsch Collection, 133. *Super Stock:* Digital Vision Ltd., 13; Larry Prosor, 14; Richard Cummins, 32; Big Cheese Photo, 46; Brian Lawrence, 108. *Getty Images:* Grant Faint, 19; Joe McBride, 48; Lisa Peardon, 64. *Smithsonian American Art Museum, Washington, DC/Art Resource, NY:* 28. *The Image Works:* John Nordell, 24; Joe Sohm, 26, 99; Francisco Rangel, 49; Geri Engberg, 53, 79; Elizabeth Crews, 58; Lou Demmatteus, 60. *Gary Conner/Index Stock:* 52. *Roger Sherman/Envision:* 80. *Tim Fitzharris/Minden Pictures:* 115.

Series redesign by Adam Mietlowski

Printed in China
1 3 5 6 4 2

Contents

California Is . . .

"Somewhere between expectation and experience exists a place, or series of places, called California. . . . California has never been allowed to be merely a state in the Union: it is also a state of mind."
—*Many Californias: Literature from the Golden State*

"There is science, logic, reason; there is thought verified by experience. And then there is California."
—writer Edward Abbey

"Hollywood's a place where they'll pay you a thousand dollars for a kiss, and fifty cents for your soul. I know, because I turned down the first offer often enough and held out for the fifty cents."
—actress Marilyn Monroe

California is a place where . . .

". . . people come to make their fortunes . . . where beautiful women are 'discovered' in drug stores, and a man can turn a mouse into an empire."
—writer M. G. Lord in *Forever Barbie*

". . . the mind is troubled by some . . . suspicion that things had better work here, because here, beneath that immense bleached sky, is where we run out of continent."
—novelist Joan Didion

California is people.

"I guess it's . . . snobbery. . . . It has something to do with just spending money. . . . The way I look at it, I can buy myself anything I can afford. We're just fast livers out here in California."
—business executive Elliot Sopkin,
on buying an expensive custom stereo for his car

"Californians are a race of people; they are not merely inhabitants of a state."
—writer O. Henry

California is dearly loved . . .

"Cross a time zone or two. Say the word, *California*. Watch the reactions. The sweet look of memories and wishes crosses [people's] faces. . . . [t]hey'll tell you about relatives who moved West. About tawny sunsets over the ocean. About the glitter . . . of the big cities and the rugged quiet of the mountains. About stars, and money won and lost, and dreams left far behind."   —newspaper columnist Anita Creamer

. . . and passionately disliked.

"The people are unreal. The flowers are unreal, they don't smell. The fruit is unreal, it doesn't taste of anything. The whole place is a glaring, gaudy, night-marish set, built upon the desert."

—actress Ethel Barrymore

For years California's major export to the rest of the country has not been its fruits and vegetables; it has been craziness. It comes in many forms—bad TV shows, bad architecture, junk foods, auto worship and creepy life-styles. . . . You name it: If it babbles and its eyeballs are glazed, it probably comes from California."

—newspaper columnist Mike Royko

California is one of those places that can be different things to different people. To residents, it is home—a place like any other, where real people lead real lives. To out-siders, it is the stuff of make-believe—Disneyland and movie stars and millionaires.

Even its history has a storybook quality. Its road to statehood did not begin with sturdy pioneers in search of land. It began with fortune hunters in search of gold.

The California gold rush of 1848–1849 set off an historic population boom. California grew so quickly that it became a state by 1850, skipping the usual process of first becoming a territory. Today it is the most populous state in the Union, with more than 35 million people. Its economy is rated fifth in the world, outranking many small nations.

Chapter One

The Lay of the Land

On the map, California looks something like a boomerang: long and narrow, curving about one-third of the way down. It has the highest and lowest places in the lower forty-eight states: Mount Whitney at 14,495 feet above sea level and Death Valley at 282 feet below.

Once, the northern mountains were active volcanoes, and the low deserts of the south were covered by an ancient sea. Glaciers carved deep river canyons into the western face of the Sierra Nevada. The San Andreas Fault slipped and slid and folded onto itself, endlessly changing and shaping the coastal lands into what we today call California.

REGIONS OF PLENTY

California is a large state measuring 770 miles at its greatest distance, from north to south. It contains ten distinct natural regions—more than any other state. Six of these regions are mountainous; three are deserts; and one is a great, fertile valley located in the center of the state.

Shimmering water cascades down a rock face at one of the state's most prized outdoor areas—Yosemite National Park.

In the northwestern corner of the state, the heavily forested Klamath Mountains reach elevations of 8,000 feet. This range includes the soaring Trinity Alps, which were carved by ancient glaciers. To the east lies the volcanic Cascade Range. Its tallest peak, Mount Shasta, is the cone of a long-dormant volcano. Mount Lassen, about 85 miles to the southeast, is one of only two volcanoes that have erupted in the twentieth century in the continental United States. Mount Lassen last erupted in 1921.

The Coast Ranges follow the Pacific shoreline from the Klamath Mountains down to Point Conception. They average from 2,000 to 4,000 feet in elevation. The northern sections are covered with trees and dotted with fertile valleys. In the south, forest gives way to chaparral, dense brush that grows in semiarid conditions.

The San Andreas Fault, a fracture in the Earth's crust, cuts through the Coast Ranges. This makes the area prone to earthquakes. There are hundreds of faults lining California; the San Andreas is simply the largest and best known. It is about 600 miles long and up to 1 mile wide.

In the eastern part of the state lies the towering Sierra Nevada range. It is an impressive barrier, 50 to 80 miles wide and stretching for about 400 miles from north to south. Along the western slopes are deep river canyons such as Yosemite Valley. The foothills are rich in mineral deposits, including gold. It was there that the gold rush of 1849 began.

Farther south are the Transverse and Peninsular ranges. The Transverse Ranges, also called the Los Angeles Ranges, define the Southern California landscape; all land routes from the north and east pass through them. Major passes include Gaviota, Cajon, Tejon, and San Gorgonio. The Peninsular Ranges, also called the San Diego Ranges, rise in the southwest and extend south into Baja, or lower,

Rock climbers have set up a winter camp below Basin Mountain in the Sierra Nevada range.

California, which is part of Mexico. Clearly, California suffers from no lack of dizzying heights.

The Central Valley

This oval valley, which runs down the center of California, is one of the most fertile agricultural areas in the world. The rich valley soil is washed down from the surrounding mountains, making it excellent for many crops from cotton, grains, nuts, rice, and fruits to all kinds of vegetables.

The valley is an everyday kind of place. Sophisticates from the coastal cities have found it an area hard to warm up to. After Ronald Reagan was elected governor of California, his wife, Nancy, had only one thing to say about living in Sacramento: "Thank heavens we can escape to Beverly Hills on the weekends."

The Deserts

Part of the huge area known as the Great Basin lies along the Nevada border. As it reaches into northern California, the basin turns into a treeless highland dotted with lava beds. The southeastern portion includes Death Valley, which extends 140 miles through eastern California and western Nevada.

To the south and east of this basin are the Colorado and Mojave deserts. The Mojave is largely barren, with great pastel vistas that seem to stretch on forever. "This place can seem grim by daylight," says one longtime resident. "Come sunset, though . . . nothing's prettier in all the world." The Colorado is made up of the Coachella and Imperial valleys, areas that have been irrigated to provide excellent farmland.

THE CLIMATE

With such wide variety of landforms, it is not surprising that California also has many different climates. The highest temperature ever recorded

The stark landscape of Death Valley suggests a far-distant planet.

in the state is 134 degrees Fahrenheit; the lowest, minus 45. There are five separate climate zones in California, called coastal, valley, foothill, mountain, and desert.

On the Southern California coast, the beaches are sunny and the winters mild. In the north, the weather tends to be colder. San Francisco is famous for its coastal breezes and the fog that rolls in from the ocean. Even in summer, mornings and evenings are "sweater weather." As Mark Twain supposedly once said: "The coldest winter I ever spent was a summer I spent in San Francisco."

The climate of the Sacramento and San Joaquin valleys is hot and dry in the summer, cold and humid in the winter. Valley winters are noted for the ground-hugging tule fog that occurs in marshy areas. (*Tule* is an Aztec word for "marsh vegetation.") This fog does not come in from the ocean, like the fog in San Francisco; tule fog seems to rise from the ground, turning everything a soft, silvery gray. "You don't drive through this stuff," says a long-haul truck driver. "You sit 'til it decides to be over." In the foothills, temperatures are similar to those in the valleys, but there are no tule fogs. Snow is also an uncommon sight.

In the mountains, summers are warm and winters are rainy, with heavy snow at the higher elevations. The Sierra Nevada, for example, get an average of 445 inches of snow each year. Californians watch each season's snowpack with avid interest; it is an important source of water. When it melts in the spring, it flows into the rivers and streams that carry water to the lowlands.

California's avid skiers welcome the arrival of winter. Thrill seekers flock to some of the state's high-altitude peaks.

In the desert, the atmosphere has so little humidity that even when the temperature reaches more than 100 degrees, the days are still bearable. As desert dwellers are fond of saying, it is a dry heat, meaning that it is less punishing than the heat that comes with high humidity. Desert nights are usually cool and pleasant, even in summer. Winter nights can plunge to sub-zero temperatures.

THE WATERWAYS

California's principal rivers are the Sacramento in the north and the San Joaquin in the south. Most of the other large rivers in the state flow into one of these two. In the south, the Colorado River flows down from the Rocky Mountains to form California's southeastern border.

California has relatively few natural lakes. The largest body of freshwater entirely within the state is Clear Lake, some 100 miles north of San Francisco. Lake Tahoe, which is larger, is located partly in Nevada. Other natural lakes are Goose, Eagle, and Mono, all in the northern part of the state.

The Salton Sea, in the desert of the Imperial Valley, was once the bed of an ancient lake. In 1905 the Colorado River flooded, filling the basin and creating an inland sea that lies about 230 feet below sea level. Because the Salton Sea has no natural outlets, water that flows into it is trapped there. Over the years, that water has become almost as salty as the ocean itself.

Most of California's freshwater lakes are actually reservoirs. Water has always been a problem in California: the northern part of the state has plenty of it, while the southern part does not. Southern California gets only 30 percent of the state's annual rainfall but uses 80 percent of the water supply. Lakes Shasta, Berryessa, Folsom, Isabella, Cachuma,

Surrounded by a sea of conifers, or cone-bearing trees, Emerald Bay in Lake Tahoe glistens like a jewel.

and Arrowhead are just a few of the better-known reservoirs. From these artificial lakes, a vast system of aqueducts moves the water to where it is needed.

CELEBRATING SWALLOWS

Every year on March 19, thousands of people gather in Southern California to witness a small miracle: the return of the swallows to San Juan Capistrano. Legend says they all arrive on that one day. Science says there is nothing special about the nineteenth, since swallows arrive throughout the month of March.

Californians ignore the experts. For more than sixty years, a joyous festival has marked the day of the swallows' return. The town patriarch rings the mission bells to welcome the migrants home. Mariachi bands stroll through the crowd—trumpets, guitars, and voices combining in exuberant Mexican songs. Brightly costumed dancers perform in the square.

Every now and then, a single voice will rise over the noise of the crowd—"I see one!"—prompting everyone to look up. The sighting may be a pigeon or a seagull; then again, it could be the first swallow of the season. Amid the music and laughter and general commotion, the festival continues. Sooner or later, someone will spot that first swallow. In the meantime, there's plenty to do and see at this annual tribute to a genuine California legend.

LAND AND WATER

Yreka

Weed · Alturas

Goose Lake

Arcata

Eureka

Shasta Lake

Cape Mendocino

Redding

Lassen Volcanic NP

Susanville

Red Bluff

Sacramento R.

Chico

Paradise

Ukiah

Williams

Yuba City

Clear L.

Santa Rosa

Woodland

Lake Tahoe

Lake Berryessa

Sacramento

Pt. Reyes

Berkeley

Stockton

San Francisco · Oakland

San Jose

San Joaquin R.

Modesto

Turlock

Mono Lake

Monterey Bay

Salinas

Merced

Monterey

Fresno

Mount Whitney (14,494 ft)

Death Valley

Visalia

Tulare

Porterville

Paso Robles

Tulare Lake

San Luis Obispo

Buena Vista Lake Bed

Bakersfield

Ridgecrest

Mojave Desert

Baker

Santa Maria

Mojave

Barstow

Lompoc

Ludlow

Pt. Conception

Santa Barbara

Lancaster

Mojave Desert

Santa Barbara Channel

Oxnard

Pasadena

San Bernardino

Santa Rosa I.

Santa Cruz I.

Los Angeles

Riverside

Long Beach

Santa Ana

Indio

Santa Catalina I.

Temecula

Palm Springs

Blythe

Oceanside

Gulf of Santa Catalina

Escondido

Salton Sea (235 ft Below Sea Level)

San Clemente I.

San Diego

El Centro

Yuma

Calexico

California's plant and animal life is as varied as the land it occupies. In the coastal woodlands of the north, giant redwoods stand as tall as 370 feet and live for more than two thousand years. Another redwood species, the famed giant sequoia of the Sierra Nevada, has an even longer life span: about three thousand years. The bristlecone pine of the east-central mountains is the oldest of all. One tree in the Inyo National Forest is 4,600 years old.

It takes several people to make a human chain around one of the state's mighty redwoods.

Oak, aspen, eucalyptus, and palm are closely associated with California. Black oak and aspen grow in the mountains, while eucalyptus and canyon live oak are found throughout the state. Scrub oak and palm appear in the south.

Other California vegetation includes myrtle and flowering dogwood in the mountains, and the golden poppy—the state flower—which once spread over the foothills and valleys of the state. The Mojave Desert is home to many kinds of drought-resistant succulents, which are fleshy plants that store water in their tissues.

Each of California's environments has its resident wildlife. The desert is home to bighorn sheep, wild burros, coyotes, hares, and many kinds of lizards. Chaparral areas host rabbits, rattlesnakes, rodents, and deer; while the mountains house cougars and bears.

Beneath the surface of rivers and lakes swim salmon, bass, and trout. The state's coastal waters support a wealth of shellfish, perch, and tuna. Marine mammals such as seals, sea lions, otters, and dolphins also make their home off the California coast.

An amazing variety of birds lives in the state or makes it a stop on their migratory rounds. Seagulls, pelicans, and terns live along the coast; spotted owls in the forests of the north; rare California condors in the Transverse Ranges of the south. Quail flourish in all areas of the state.

In the central-valley town of Colusa, anyone who finds an abandoned nest takes the eggs to farmer Roger Moore. For thirty years, Moore has run a volunteer hatchery for ducks, pheasants, marsh hawks, valley quail—any kind of bird that happens his way. He cares for the hatchlings until they can survive on their own. "It just takes a little work," Moore says, "or make that a lot of work by a lot of people, but it's worth it."

A brown pelican keeps watch along the California coast. A local species is currently endangered in the state.

THE PEOPLE

California is the most populous state in the nation, with an estimated 35.1 million people in 2002. More than 91 percent of them live in the densely populated urban areas along the coast. The five counties that make up Southern California have more people than the state's other fifty-three counties combined.

The difference is quite dramatic. For example, Del Norte County, which borders Oregon in the northwest, has a population of only 27,482; San Diego County, which borders Mexico in the southwest, has 2,906,660 people. The San Francisco Bay area, which is the major metropolitan center of the north, has fewer than two million people. Greater Los Angeles, the southern population center, has nearly nine million.

Geography and weather account for much of this population pattern. The northernmost part of the state is mountainous, with thin soil and difficult terrain. Its coastline is rugged and rocky; its weather, cold and rainy. The south has flatland ideal for building and farming, as well as white sand beaches that stretch from Santa Barbara to San Diego and a mild climate that permits year-round agriculture. People were just naturally drawn to that part of the state.

Farther inland, the southern deserts were sparsely populated until improved irrigation and water-transport systems made it possible for people to live and work there. In the 1980s and 1990s, thousands left the metropolitan Los Angeles area in search of cleaner air and lower housing costs. Many of them continued to commute to their jobs, driving great distances on crowded freeways. "The only way we could afford a decent house was to move out here to the boondocks," says a mechanic who lives 50 miles from his workplace.

SAVING THE CALIFORNIA CONDOR

When rancher Eben McMillan first settled in San Luis Obispo County, he got used to the big shadows that crossed his lawn every day at lunchtime. When he looked up, he would see majestic black condors outlined against the sky. Condors are the largest land bird in North America, with an average weight of 20 pounds and a wingspan of 9 to 10 feet. There were hundreds of them back in the 1940s when Eben bought his land. By 1982 fewer than two dozen remained.

Environmentalists began a habitat-restoration and captive-breeding program. Ten years later, the total condor population was up to sixty-three, with fifty-six of them still living in captivity. A massive program to return condors to the wild had its ups and downs. Captive-bred birds had no fear of humans and no knowledge of hazards such as power lines

Animal behavior experts went to work. They taught condors not to land on power poles by setting up fake poles that gave mild shocks. Professional trainers deliberately harassed the birds so they would learn to avoid humans.

Every release of young birds into the wild is a major event for the Condor Recovery Team. Each bird within the group has an individual code. It is formed from the first letter of the color code, along with a personal number. For example, a red tag means that the bird belongs to a group released on September 12, 2002. The code R32 allows workers to track the entire life history of that particular bird.

Young condors are first sent to a release facility. They live in a huge pen while they adapt to the area and learn how to survive in the wild. The year 2003 made history at Pinnacles National Monument in central California. In September seven male condors moved into a brand-new release facility. By December they were ready for freedom. When these birds took wing, they became the first condors at Pinnacles in more than one hundred years.

Smog is a familiar sight to Los Angeles commuters. Southern California's large population results in heavy and frequent traffic jams and higher levels of air pollution.

Ever since California became a state, it has experienced rapid population growth, as much as 50 percent in some years. During the 1980s, for example, California's overall population grew at a rate of more than 25 percent. This rapid rise has taken its toll on the environment. For decades, residents of Los Angeles have coped with the brownish haze that hangs in the air on windless days. It was first dubbed smog (combining parts of the words *SMoke* and *fOG*) in 1905, and the name stuck. At the time, smog was something of a joke. It was bad, yes, but most people did not realize how bad.

By the 1990s nobody was laughing. Smog has become a problem across the state. Efforts to clean up the air center on controlling automobile emissions. This is not an easy task, because Californians love their cars. Long commutes in bumper-to-bumper traffic have become the norm. Responses to pollution include smog-control devices on cars and trucks, unleaded gasoline, and the development of public-transit systems.

A twenty-first-century project with great promise is the Zero Emissions Vehicle (ZEV). ZEVs are powered by electricity, alternate fuels such as hydrogen, fuel cells, or superclean gas. The most popular and practical of them are hybrids—vehicles that use a combination of electricity and clean-burning gasoline.

The California legislature has offered several incentives to buyers of ZEVs. These include reduced licensing fees and protected parking at charging facilities for all-electric vehicles. Many bridges exempt ZEVs from tolls. In a state where bridge tolls average two to three dollars per round-trip crossing, that can amount to substantial savings for commuters.

Many Californians work hard to protect the natural life of the Golden State and to ensure it has a bright future. Here, woman take part in cleanup efforts at Huntington Beach.

A regulation set forth by California's Air Resources Board will ensure that ZEVs are available to the state's consumers. In 2003 all automakers selling in California had to produce a minimum of 4,450 electric cars and 100,000 other clean vehicles.

Air quality receives a great deal of attention from California's state government, but it is certainly not the only concern. Another important goal is protecting the state's coastal waters. Offshore oil drilling became a major issue in 1969. An oil platform blowout coated more than 35 miles of California's coast with a 660-square-mile mat of black tar.

Californians never forgot the lesson of that ecological disaster. When the federal government tried to renew offshore leases with oil companies, California went to court. In June 2001, a U.S. district court ruled that the state had the right to ban drilling. On December 3, 2002, a federal appeals court upheld the decision. Governor Gray Davis called the decision "a big stop sign to Washington." He called on the federal government to stop trying to "exploit California's . . . coastal resources."

California's concern for the environment has made it a leader in protecting natural resources. There are programs to protect forests, deserts, wildlife, lakes, and rivers. Recycling has become a way of life, reducing the demand on landfills. Some of the programs are small and local, while others are large and statewide. Each reflects California's determination to protect its natural resources for today as well as for tomorrow.

Chapter Two

California Yesterdays

Spanish explorers first entered California in 1542. Missionaries followed, building a chain of twenty-one churches along what became known as *El Camino Real*, or "the Royal Road." California was part of Mexico until the Treaty of Guadalupe Hidalgo ceded it to the United States in 1848.

That same year, gold was discovered at John Sutter's mill, in the Sierra foothills. Fortune hunters swarmed over the area, chasing their dreams and adding their deeds to California's rich history. They paved the way for many adventurous souls to come.

NATIVE INHABITANTS

The native peoples of California built no cities, crowned no kings, and made no formal laws. They lived off the land, gathering and eating nuts, seeds, roots, and berries. Mountain tribes hunted deer and small game. Coastal tribes harvested fish and shellfish from the ocean.

Though the tribes were not unified into a nation, they did have a great deal in common. They lived in comfortable huts or tepees made of

California was home to many native groups that spread across the state. This painting from the 1870s shows Indians at a council meeting, a gathering in which native leaders met and discussed important matters.

The coming of white settlers forever changed the native way of life. These native Californians canoe in San Francisco Bay. Its coastline is marked by one of the state's famed missions.

local materials: redwood bark in the north, brush in the chaparral country, tule in the wetlands of the river deltas.

They forged rich cultural traditions. People sang songs while they went about their daily tasks and told stories around evening campfires. The Pomo of northern California were skilled basket makers. They could weave straw so tightly that the basket could hold water. The Chumash of

Southern California created elaborate cave paintings that were probably connected with their religious rituals.

California tribes tended to be small. For example, in the 1840s the Yana of northern California had just a few thousand members. The related Yahi included only four hundred. Though their languages belonged to the same family, the Yana and Yahi could not really communicate with each another.

This fact became important in the famous case of Ishi, the last of the Yahi people. In August 1911, Ishi was found in the foothills near Mount Lassen in northern California. His entire family had died, one by one. For three years, Ishi had survived without human company.

When he came into the white world, his first problem was communication. No living person could speak his language. Sam Balwi, an English-speaking Yana, tried to communicate with Ishi. The two men could guess at a few words in each other's language, but they could not carry on a conversation. Anthropologists Alfred Kroeber and Thomas Waterman taught Ishi English and learned some Yahi as well along the way.

For five years, Ishi lived and worked at the anthropology museum in San Francisco. By the time he died of tuberculosis in 1916, he had honored his own culture and enriched California's. The Yahi people and their story became a permanent part of the state's history.

EXPLORERS AND MISSIONARIES

The area that is now California was discovered in 1542 by Juan Rodríguez Cabrillo. He was a Portuguese-born sailor who served under Hernán Cortés. Cabrillo sailed north from Mexico to find a Northwest Passage that would connect the Atlantic and Pacific oceans. Instead, he found California.

California's twenty-one missions stand as powerful reminders of the state's Spanish heritage.

He thought he had found a dream. A popular adventure story of the day told of a fabulous island in the western sea. It was inhabited by Amazon warriors and ruled by a queen named Calafia. The explorers may have named the new land in her honor.

California was a wondrous place. It had abundant resources and no armies to protect them. The conquistadors, or conquerors, set out to possess this land. Missionaries followed, determined to convert native tribes to Christianity. During that period, the famous California missions sprang up, from San Diego in the south (founded in 1769) to Sonoma in the north (founded in 1823).

THE CALIFORNIOS

After the missionaries came the Californios: aristocrats who held vast territories under Spanish land grants. They led gracious and privileged lives. Like European nobility, the Californios cultivated swordsmanship, horsemanship, and the social graces. Work was for servants and laborers.

Life was very different for the less than wealthy. They had little choice but to work for the *patrón*, or boss, who had almost total control of their lives. In Southern California, three powerful families owned most of the usable land: the Carrillos, with 320,000 acres; the de la Guerras, with 326,000; and the Picos, with 532,000. Northern California was divided among the Alvarados, Castros, Peraltas, and Vallejos.

The fortunes of the Californios changed after the Mexican-American War of 1846–1848. Mexico lost the war and on February 2, 1848, ceded California to the United States. The timing could not have been better for the Americans, or worse for the Spanish noblemen. Just a week before the treaty was signed, a man named James Marshall discovered gold at Sutter's Mill.

When California became an American possession, fortune hunters from the East and Midwest flooded into gold country. Instant towns sprang into being—rough settlements with names such as Greenhorn Bar, Humbug Hill, and Whiskey Flat. They were lawless places, where life was often rough and expensive. Merchants sold food, clothing, and mining supplies at inflated prices. Women could make small fortunes just taking in laundry or preparing home-cooked meals.

A GOLD RUSH LAUNDRY

In 1849 pioneer doctor Felix Wierzbicki wrote of his experiences in gold country in *The Californians*. He devoted a great deal of attention to the subject of laundry. It was a real problem for the forty-niners, the men who had come in search of gold, because washing clothes was "woman's work" and there were few women in the gold towns:

The greatest privation that a bachelor [faces] is not being able to furnish himself with clean linen when he desires, as domestic service is so difficult to be kept up here for want of working women. To induce some of the few women that are here . . . to wash their linen for them, they have to court them besides paying six dollars a dozen.

According to Wierzbicki, one forty-niner "paid" for his laundry with a marriage proposal, "because she refused to wash his clothes for him [otherwise]."

Fortune hunters known as forty-niners came to California, starting in the late 1840s, in search of gold.

People came by land and by sea. They crossed the Sierras on foot, on horseback, or in covered wagons. They sailed around Cape Horn and up the coast. In a few months, San Francisco grew from a sleepy village to a metropolitan port. There, fortune hunters docked before making their way to gold country.

They all dreamed of great riches. Many returned with their dreams in shambles. Others did not return at all. For every story of fame and fortune, there were ten of heartbreak and death. People died of exposure, disease, and accident. Some were mauled by the fierce grizzly bears that roamed the foothills. Some took their own lives after failing to strike gold. Many fell victim to foul play, as gold fever turned would-be millionaires into claim jumpers and killers.

"Since my arrival here," wrote forty-niner William Perkins, "three Mexicans and one [American] have been killed in street fights." Another forty-niner recorded the anonymous funerals of many of the gold seekers: "It is an everyday occurrence to see a coffin carried on the shoulders of two men, who are the only mourners and only witnesses of the burial of some stranger they do not know."

For good or ill, the gold rush shaped California society. The hardy dreamers who came west were not the sort to live by ordinary rules. They liked excitement, and they liked taking chances. Schemes and dreams became a way of life. By the time California became a state in 1850, it was already *El Dorado*, the gilded one, a place where the pursuit of happiness was everybody's most cherished right.

THE BIG FOUR

Even after the gold rush, California remained the fastest-growing state in the nation. By the turn of the century, it had a population of close to 1,500,000, up from less than 100,000 in 1850. The completion of the transcontinental railroad in 1869 made the westward journey faster and less dangerous.

The "Big Four" who built the western railroad were Charles Crocker, Mark Hopkins, Collis P. Huntington, and Leland Stanford. They began as Sacramento businessmen, prosperous but far from rich. Huntington and Hopkins operated a hardware and mining supply store; Crocker was a dry-goods merchant; Stanford, a lawyer. None of them knew anything about railroading. What they did know was how to promote an idea.

The transcontinental railroad was just the kind of visionary scheme they liked. They started with $6,000 and a half-formed idea. On the strength of their daring, the Central Pacific Railroad issued $8,500,000 of stock on the strength of that $6,000 of start-up money.

Collis Huntington convinced Congress to give the railroad $25 million worth of

Chinese laborers, using picks and shovels, turn their attention to a long railroad trestle in this photograph from 1877.

BANKS OF THE SACRAMENTO

This sea shanty was sung by sailors who took the *Flying Cloud,* the fastest clipper ship in the Black Ball line, on the dangerous route around Cape Horn to the California gold fields.

Music by Stephen Foster ("Camptown Races")

Lyrics (melody line):

In the Black Ball Line I served my time, With a hoo-dah, With a hoo-dah; In a full-rigged ship, and in her prime, with a hoo-dah,. hoo-dah day.

Chorus

So blow, blow,_ blow for Cal - i - for - ni - o. There's plen-ty of gold, so I've been told, On the banks of the Sac - ra - men - to.

government bonds and 4.5 million acres of public land. When the time came to hire a contractor to do the actual building, the Big Four set up their own construction company and hired themselves. Charles Crocker headed the construction company, and he took his work seriously: "Why, I used to go up and down that road in my car like a mad bull," he once said, "stopping along wherever there was anything amiss, and raising Old Nick with the boys that were not up to time."

Work crews laid almost 1,200 miles of track, starting from Sacramento and going over the Sierras to Promontory, Utah. There, the eastern and western lines joined. By that time, construction costs were over budget, the Big Four were millionaires, and the railroad was in debt. In spite of all that, the transcontinental railroad brought new jobs, new markets—and new people—into California. Some came to make their fortunes; others came to find homes.

HOORAY FOR HOLLYWOOD

In the early years of the twentieth century, moviemakers found both a new home and new fortunes in California. In the process, they transformed a sleepy little town called Hollywood into the glamour capitol of the world.

The motion-picture industry actually began in New York City, but outdoor filming was often impossible during the winter months. What the movie pioneers needed was a land of endless summer and stunning landscapes. Southern California fit the bill.

Director D. W. Griffith is generally credited with transforming motion pictures from a passing fad into a thriving industry. Other filmmakers just placed the camera in front of a staging area and let it run. Griffith used it the way an artist uses brushes and paints: as a tool for shaping his ideas. He put the camera on a rolling platform so he could move it around; created per-

The legendary director D. W. Griffith watches actors perform a scene, as the cameraman captures all the action. This behind-the-scenes view was taken in 1918. The motion-picture industry was drawn to Southern California's warm and steady climate and established permanent roots in Los Angeles.

spective with long, medium, and close-up shots; changed scenes with fade-ins and fade-outs; and created moods with angled shots and soft focus.

He also "invented" the movie star. In the earliest films, actors received neither screen credit nor pay for their work. Griffith put their names on the screen and transformed them into living legends. People lined up to see the latest Mary Pickford or Charlie Chaplin movie and scoured magazines and newspapers for gossip about the private lives of the stars. This kind of fame took its toll. Hollywood was not an easy or forgiving place:

"To survive there," said actress Billie Burke, "you need the ambition of a Latin American revolutionary, the ego of a grand opera tenor, and the physical stamina of a cow pony."

By the 1920s, the name *Hollywood* had taken on magical associations. Like the mother lode of the forty-niners, it became part of the California dream. After the stock market crash of 1929, thousands of desperate Americans looked to that dream to boost their sagging spirits.

A GARDEN OF EDEN

The Depression-era immigrants were not looking for gold or hoping to become movie stars; they were just trying to survive. Nearly a million displaced sharecroppers came from the prairie states during the Great

During the Great Depression, a train trip was a luxury few could afford. These men are traveling to Los Angeles the only way they can—by foot.

Depression. They lost their money to failed banks and their land to dust storms that killed crops and stripped away the topsoil.

They came west in broken-down jalopies, with all their possessions piled into the trunks, strapped on top, and shoved into every nook and cranny of the cars. They had heard that California had plenty of work and so much food it was free for the picking in fields and orchards across the state. They soon learned the truth: ten or twenty people applied for every low-paying job, and nobody gave away food—or anything else—for free.

CALIFORNIA ON THE CUTTING EDGE

After the Depression, California continued to grow in population and influence. During World War II, California's military installations were

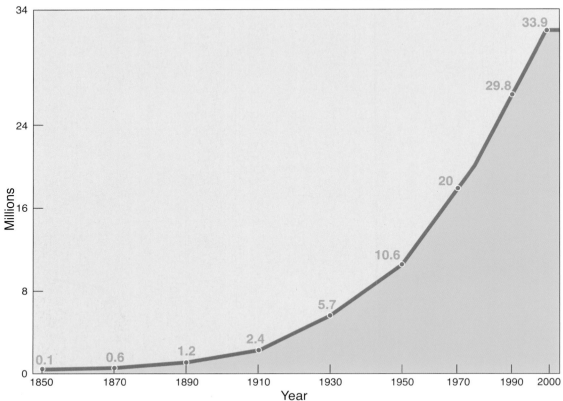

POPULATION GROWTH: 1850–2000

Millions

0.1 — 1850
0.6 — 1870
1.2 — 1890
2.4 — 1910
5.7 — 1930
10.6 — 1950
20 — 1970
29.8 — 1990
33.9 — 2000

Year

the staging area for American forces in the Pacific. In the 1960s, its college campuses produced a generation of young activists who protested the war in Vietnam, marched for civil rights, and formed a free-speech movement that spread to colleges all over the country.

In the 1970s, California remained on the cutting edge of social and political activism. Californians championed the women's liberation movement and Native American rights. They helped to create the personal growth, or New Age, movement.

Thousands of Californians experimented with everything from meditation to organic foods and natural healing. They attended seminars and workshops, read books, and formed self-help groups. Many New Age Californians valued spiritual and psychological growth over economic success. They stressed simple living as an alternative to the earn-and-spend consumer culture of the times.

The focus shifted in the 1980s, as California helped to lead the way into the computer age. Among the cultural heroes of the decade were high-tech visionaries. They transformed society with technology such as the personal computer (PC), the videocassette recorder (VCR), and the compact disk (CD).

In addition to chanting and meditating, these people at Mount Shasta raise their hands to celebrate a favorable arrangement of the planets. Starting mostly in the 1970s, New Age spirituality found avid support among many Golden State residents.

Steve Jobs, for example, has become something of a living legend. Jobs grew up in the part of northern California now known as Silicon Valley. In 1976 he cofounded Apple Computer. By the 1980s, Apple was on its way to becoming a multimillion-dollar company. Several computer-related companies moved into the area. Some made components, or parts, to be assembled into computers. Others made software, the programming that directs the computer to perform specific tasks.

By the 1990s, the Internet was coming into its own. Again, California was on the cutting edge. Dozens of "dot-com" companies formed to do business over the Internet. Silicon Valley and the San Francisco Bay area became home to a new crop of "overnight" millionaires and highly paid technical workers and executives.

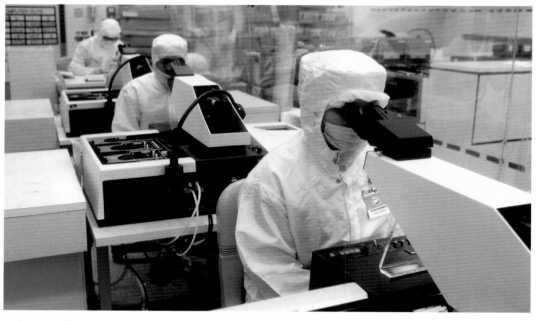

Silicon Valley, south of the San Francisco Bay area, established itself as one of the world's major technological centers.

This new prosperity left many Californians behind. The gap between rich and poor widened. Average families were priced out of home ownership. Many could not even afford to rent a decent apartment. At the lowest end of the economic ladder, homelessness became a problem.

The state government had to cope with this growing poverty. It also had to prepare for wave upon wave of immigration. Throughout the 1980s and into the 1990s, immigrants and refugees from other countries poured into California. Many needed help, from affordable housing to medical care, English classes, and job training.

INTO THE NEW CENTURY

California began the twenty-first century facing a new set of problems. The dot-com boom collapsed. Companies went out of business. People who had become used to their newfound wealth suddenly found themselves jobless and broke.

While the economy was reeling from this blow, an energy crisis hit the state. Power companies could not generate enough electricity to keep up with the growing demand. Rolling blackouts—periods when power was deliberately cut off in certain areas—became commonplace. The state government had to buy power from outside suppliers. This emergency power was so expensive that it drained the state treasury and created a financial crisis.

A state born in the great gold rush of 1849 knows about boom-and-bust economies. In good times and bad, California has been a magnet for people seeking their fortune: gold hunters, railroad tycoons, movie moguls, and high-tech dreamers. They were risk takers, and they created a society that is resilient, able to bounce back from troubled times. This legacy of survival is history's gift to the present and the future of the Golden State.

Chapter Three

Living Together

Much has been written about the California lifestyle. According to modern legend, everyone in the state is young, blond, and gorgeous. They live on salads, salsa, and guacamole, wear the latest designer sportswear; and spend their time shopping, surfing, or lying around on the beach. Every second or third person on the street is a movie star or a rock singer.

The real California is not nearly so glamorous—but it is even more interesting. California has many kinds of people who live in many different ways. There is a large Armenian community in Fresno, a Pakistani settlement near Sacramento, and a thriving Sikh temple in Yuba City. Filipinos and other Pacific Islanders live in many communities up and down the coast. The three largest minority groups are Latinos, Asians, and African Americans.

For most of the twentieth century, whites were an overwhelming majority in the state. That changed in 1999. For the first time in history, non-Latino whites accounted for less than 50 percent of the state's population. The combined number of Latinos, Asians, and African Americans became greater than the number of whites.

When many outsiders think of the state, clichéd images of the supposed California lifestyle often spring to mind. According to the modern legend, the state is filled with young, fashionable, socially conscious people.

That trend has continued into the twenty-first century. Whites have become the largest minority in a state of minorities. Some feel threatened by this diversity. Others feel enriched by it. Each racial, ethnic, and religious group adds its special touches to California culture.

Mexican Americans and other Latinos make up the second-largest minority group in California and are more than 31 percent of the total population. In 1910 they accounted for only 2 percent of the state's 2,377,549 people. That percentage began to grow during the Mexican Revolution. Between 1910 and 1915, thousands of Mexicans came north to escape the war and to find work in California agriculture. They lived in barrios, which in Spanish means "neighborhoods," and worked in the fields.

Over the years, Mexican immigrants mixed their traditions with American ones to create a new Mexican-American culture. They had their own way of dressing and speaking, their own fads and cultural values. Many were fully bilingual in Spanish and

California's residents are drawn to the state's diversity and its wealth of wide-open spaces.

English. The neighborhood and the family played important roles in the lives of Mexican Americans. They made their own island of belonging, in the midst of a sometimes hostile society.

In the 1960s, they began moving beyond that island. That was a time of protests and demonstrations for many causes: equal rights for minorities, peace in Southeast Asia, free speech on college campuses. Mexican Americans joined the struggle. People such as Ruben Salazar and Cesar Chavez led the fight.

Salazar was a talented writer whose pieces in the *Los Angeles Times* told the hard truth about life in the barrio. He was killed in August 1970, when a protest march exploded into violence.

Cesar Chavez tirelessly labored to improve conditions for migrant farmworkers.

Chavez was a migrant farmworker with an eighth-grade education and a dream. Migrants picked crops up and down the state, living in grim labor camps and working for starvation wages. Chavez organized them into a labor union. With strikes and rallies and boycotts, the United Farm Workers of America (UFW) won better wages and working conditions for its members.

THE SWALLOW AND THE SONGBIRD

Many California stories have a Spanish or Mexican flavor. They have color and fire and romance—and sometimes sadness. This tale is ageless:

The swallows came back as always that year. The sky over Capistrano was alive with them. A songbird, watching them arrive, chanced to notice a pretty young swallow. When she looked his way, he began to sing a fine soaring melody that touched the swallow's heart.

And just like that, the two were in love.

All summer, they were together. The songbird helped the little swallow build her nest in the eaves of the little church. Sometimes they rested there in the shadows. Sometimes they flew for the simple joy of flying, and sometimes they sat in the mesquite tree beside the mission wall.

Then came the time that both had dreaded; the time when the leaves begin to turn and autumn nips the air. "Soon I must go," said the swallow, but the songbird begged her to stay.

"The flight is long and dangerous," he said. "So many perish on the

ASIANS AND PACIFIC ISLANDERS

Asians and Pacific Islanders (Filipinos, Samoans, and others from the South Pacific) are the next largest group living in California, making up about 12 percent of the population. Of all Asian groups, the Chinese and Japanese have been in the state the longest. The Chinese came during the gold rush and stayed to build the transcontinental railroad. When the Big Four needed workers to lay the tracks, Charles Crocker decided to hire Chinese immigrants. The first all-Chinese crew of fifty men went to work *journey. Stay here with me. I'll take care of you."*

"If I stay here," replied the swallow, "I will surely die. I can't live in this place through the winter."

"Maybe I could go with you," the songbird suggested, but the swallow shook her head.

"Then you would be the one to die. You can't fly so far."

The two birds talked for a long time. Finally, they decided that the only sensible thing was for the swallow to go and the songbird to stay behind.

And so they said good-bye, vowing to meet again in the spring. The songbird waited. When the swallows returned to Capistrano, he watched the skies for his beloved. He went to the little church where she had built her nest, and he went to the mesquite tree where they had spent so many pleasant afternoons. He waited there until nightfall. He waited by starlight and by sunlight; he waited in the eaves of the church and the branches of the mesquite tree. He waited and he waited; every spring he waited. Until one day, the swallows returned and the mesquite tree was empty. The songbird waited no more.

in 1865. By the time the railroad was finished in 1869, ten thousand Chinese workers had helped to build it.

After finishing the job, the Chinese turned to agriculture, mining, and manufacturing. They lived in their own neighborhoods, establishing large Chinatowns in San Francisco, Los Angeles, and other cities.

Many modern Chinese Americans have settled in communities across the state but still keep their links to traditional Chinese culture. Each September, for example, hundreds gather in San Francisco's Chinatown

A traditional costume adds spark and flair to a parade celebrating California's rich Chinese culture.

for the Moon Festival. People dress in lavish ceremonial costumes, and the streets come alive with music and laughter. There are craft exhibitions, kung-fu demonstrations, and plenty of moon cakes to eat. The highlight of the two-day event is a traditional lion dance.

Like the Chinese, Japanese Americans in California have also kept their culture alive. Traditional Japanese culture has a way of turning ordinary activities into art forms: gardeners create wondrous landscapes from plants, stones, and sculptured wood; calligraphers turn the symbols of the Japanese language into art; even arranging flowers or serving tea is done with full attention to the task of the moment.

As a Zen Buddhist saying goes, "If you walk, just walk. If you sit, just sit; but whatever you do, don't wobble." This love of the commonplace has made Japanese arts popular with Californians of other backgrounds. Community centers and colleges all over the state teach everything from calligraphy to flower arranging.

Prominent Japanese Americans associated with California include actor George Takei of *Star Trek* fame, figure skater Kristi Yamaguchi, and orchestra conductor Seiji Ozawa.

Pacific Islanders are a growing presence in California. This woman, formerly of the Marshall Islands, teaches her seven-year-old daughter how to crochet in their backyard in Oakland.

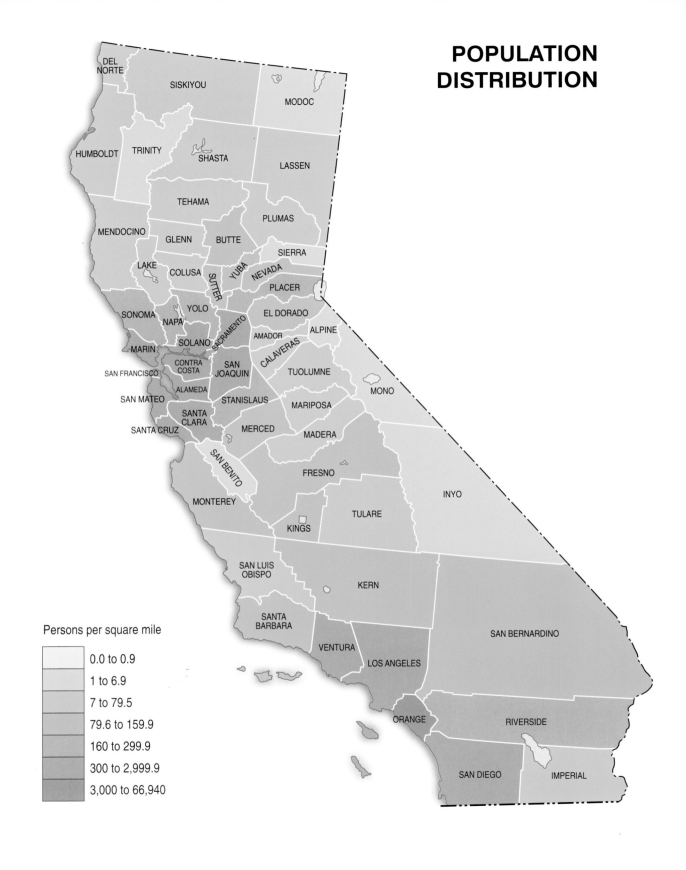

POPULATION DISTRIBUTION

Persons per square mile

- 0.0 to 0.9
- 1 to 6.9
- 7 to 79.5
- 79.6 to 159.9
- 160 to 299.9
- 300 to 2,999.9
- 3,000 to 66,940

DEL NORTE
SISKIYOU
MODOC
HUMBOLDT
TRINITY
SHASTA
LASSEN
TEHAMA
PLUMAS
MENDOCINO
GLENN
BUTTE
SIERRA
LAKE
COLUSA
SUTTER
YUBA
NEVADA
PLACER
SONOMA
YOLO
EL DORADO
NAPA
SACRAMENTO
AMADOR
ALPINE
SOLANO
CALAVERAS
MARIN
CONTRA COSTA
SAN JOAQUIN
TUOLUMNE
SAN FRANCISCO
MONO
ALAMEDA
SAN MATEO
STANISLAUS
MARIPOSA
SANTA CLARA
MERCED
MADERA
SANTA CRUZ
SAN BENITO
FRESNO
INYO
MONTEREY
TULARE
KINGS
SAN LUIS OBISPO
KERN
SANTA BARBARA
SAN BERNARDINO
VENTURA
LOS ANGELES
ORANGE
RIVERSIDE
SAN DIEGO
IMPERIAL

At the beginning of the gold rush, there were only about one thousand African Americans in California. Some were taken west as slaves, some came as free people, and some came as fugitives from a system that counted them as property. When California became a state, it outlawed slavery but kept many racist laws. African Americans could not vote, testify in court, or own property. Their children could attend only segregated schools.

In spite of these restrictions, some African Americans achieved distinction. During the first half of the nineteenth century, frontiersman James

Two friends enjoy a summer day on the streets of Long Beach.

JUNETEENTH JUBILEE

Slaves in Texas finally got the word on June 19, 1865: President Abraham Lincoln had set them free! The news was more than two years old by the time it reached Texas, but that did not matter. The former slaves rejoiced, and from that day on, they marked Juneteenth as a festival of freedom. Over the years, the custom has spread to California.

Juneteenth brings hundreds of people to Sacramento's McClatchy Park. Music is a key part of the celebration with people singing about togetherness, friendship, and freedom. Some bring guitars or harmonicas or old violins to play. The tangy smell of barbecue wafts through the air.

"It's a time when we can build tradition," says teacher Patricia Adelekan. "It's an awakening of something that's been hidden for a long time."

Not everyone knows about Juneteenth yet, but each year the Sacramento festival grows bigger and more colorful. It has become a true California holiday because it gives people a chance to celebrate freedom—and to have some fun at the same time.

Beckwourth ranged from the Rocky Mountains of Colorado to the Sierras of California. He lived among the Crow and other Native American tribes. They accepted him readily because he was a man of his word—and because he knew as well as they how difficult it was to live in a racist society. In 1850 Jim Beckwourth discovered the Sierra Nevada pass that bears his name.

Allen Allensworth was born a slave in Kentucky. In California he founded a town where African Americans could live, and work, and govern themselves. Allensworth, California, prospered for a decade but finally fell victim to the fate of many desert communities: lack of a dependable source of water. In 1976 the Department of Parks and Recreation restored his pioneering settlement as an historic park.

During World War II, African Americans flocked to California to work in shipyards, steel mills, and aircraft plants. By 1990 more than two million African Americans lived in the state.

Partly because of the prejudice they still face, some African Americans in California choose to set down roots in certain areas. The Watts neighborhood in Los Angeles and Hunter's Point in San Francisco have large African-American populations. So do the Bay Area cities of Richmond and Oakland. But African Americans are found living in cities and towns across the state.

Lisa grew up in Oakland but dreamed of living somewhere else. "It's a place you want out of," she says. She became a hairdresser and moved to a small town that is a three-hour drive from the old neighborhood. She has her own shop, where her clientele includes people of all ethnic backgrounds.

THE NEWEST CALIFORNIANS

In the 1980s and 1990s, immigrants and refugees from many cultures poured into California. According to the Immigration and Naturalization Service, more than two million legal immigrants lived in California in 2003. Another two million had entered the state illegally. These new arrivals traveled from countries far and wide and included Latinos from Colombia and Guatemala; Southeast Asians from Vietnam, Laos, and Cambodia; and refugees from the former Soviet Union.

People who have newly arrived in California from foreign lands often face a unique set of challenges. A language barrier can be among the largest. This first-grade teacher helps his young student practice writing in Spanish and English.

These new Californians face many challenges in adjusting to American life. They need job training, affordable housing, schooling for their children, and medical care.

Some arrive with serious health problems. For example, California doctors see cases of tuberculosis among some newly arrived Asians and radiation poisoning from the nuclear-power-plant failure in the Ukrainian town of Chernobyl. In some California school districts, teachers routinely face classrooms where students speak six or more different languages. Statewide, about one hundred languages can be heard spoken every day.

Providing services for immigrants is costly. Most Californians accept the expense for humanitarian reasons. Some resent it, especially when those services go to illegal immigrants. This is especially true during economic downturns.

IMMIGRATION ISSUES

The unsteady California economy of the early 1990s triggered a surge of anti-immigrant measures. In the 1994 election, voters passed Proposition 187, which denied social services to illegal aliens. It also

COMING TO CALIFORNIA: A REFUGEE'S STORY

Nally Yun, a Cambodian refugee who settled in California, escaped her homeland in 1979. After three long years in a Thai refugee camp, she made her way to the United States—and freedom. She and her husband started out with nothing but the willingness to work and a loan from a refugee organization.

In 1986 they bought a doughnut shop in Sacramento. By 1996 they owned the shop and three houses—one for themselves and two that they rented to relatives. Their four children got As and Bs in school and felt settled and comfortable in their lives in Sacramento.

In 1993 the Yuns became citizens. "It felt great," said Nally. "We know for sure we are Americans. The judge told us we are not second-class citizens. We are first class. It's really God-blessed that I am here. It's really freedom."

required teachers, health-care workers, and others to report suspected illegals to immigration authorities.

The measure sent shock waves through California's Latino communities. More illegal aliens come from Mexico, Central America, or South America than from other parts of the world. The border is close and not too difficult to pass over, so thousands cross it every year.

Most Mexican Americans considered Proposition 187 an unwelcome message sent out to all Latinos. They feared the day when a person could get reported simply for "looking Mexican" or speaking Spanish. They also resented the claim that illegal aliens come to California so they can get

Thousands of Californians were vocally opposed to the measures in Proposition 187. This rally occurred in San Francisco.

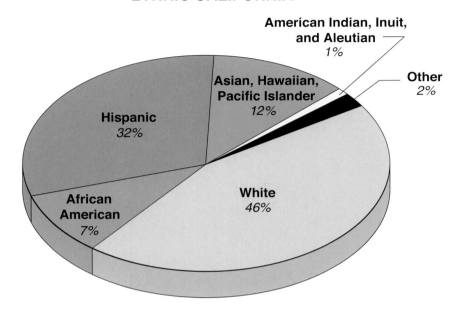

ETHNIC CALIFORNIA

American Indian, Inuit, and Aleutian
1%

Other
2%

Asian, Hawaiian, Pacific Islander
12%

Hispanic
32%

White
46%

African American
7%

welfare payments. Actually, many come to work on the state's large commercial farms.

"The Proposition 187 ads showed Mexicans running over the border, but they never showed us working in the fields," a sixteen-year-old high school student told the *Sacramento Bee.* "My family feels so discriminated against and angry."

This student's family was not alone. Opponents of Proposition 187 moved to block it in the courts. U.S. district court judge Mariana R. Pfaelzer issued an injunction. It stopped Proposition 187 from going into effect until the court could hear the case.

In 1995 Judge Pfaelzer ruled that Proposition 187 was unconstitutional. California could not withhold education, health care, or welfare benefits from undocumented immigrants. Nor could it require teachers and social-service workers to report suspected illegals to the authorities.

BEAN-AND-CHEESE BURRITOS

Most people think that burritos are a Mexican food; actually, they are a Mexican-style California food. They are also delicious and easy to make:

Ingredients:
  2 16-ounce cans Mexican-style refried beans
  6 flour tortillas
  about 1 cup finely chopped onion
  11/2 cups shredded cheddar cheese

1. Heat the beans. (Ask an adult to help you do this on the stove, in a microwave, or in a small Crock-Pot.)

2. Steam the tortillas just enough to make them warm and flexible. A microwave does this nicely. Stack the tortillas on a plate with waxed paper (NOT aluminum foil or plastic wrap) between them. Cover with a moist kitchen towel, and microwave for about 45 seconds.

3. Put about 1/2 cup of beans in a line down the center of each tortilla, leaving about 1 inch at top and bottom. Sprinkle with chopped onions (about 2 tablespoons) and shredded cheese (about 1/4 cup).

4. Fold the top and bottom and then the sides of the tortilla over the filling, sealing it inside. Your burritos are ready to eat!

Supporters of Proposition 187 appealed the ruling. A new round of court action began. It did not end until June 1999, when Governor Gray Davis made an agreement with civil-rights groups. It resolved the conflicts by removing most provisions of the measure.

In 2003 yet another 1994 law came to an end. This one denied drivers' licenses to illegal immigrants. In the interests of road safety, the legislature passed a bill that would make illegal immigrants eligible for licenses. On September 5, Governor Davis signed it into law.

A MULTICULTURAL LIFESTYLE

Alongside the problems that may set racial or ethnic groups against one another, there are signs of greater tolerance and understanding. High schools in different parts of the state have multicultural clubs, where students from different cultural, racial, and religious backgrounds come together to share their traditions. Most of these clubs leave studying for the classroom; their purpose is to share experiences. They sample each other's foods, sing each other's songs, and celebrate each other's holidays.

In many California cities, whole neighborhoods are taking on a multicultural flavor. On Stockton Boulevard in Sacramento, journalist Stephen Magagnini saw a Romanian woman buying a cake from a Chinese bakery, which rents space in a furniture store owned by a Korean and managed by a Latina.

But despite the many hopeful signs, California still has its troubles. Different racial and ethnic groups do not always get along. There are people who long for the days when whites were still a clear majority in the state, and everybody else was supposed to learn their way of doing things. There are people who worry that sharing other cultures will mean losing their own.

California is known for its vibrant, multicultural communities.

In the early twenty-first century, California stands halfway between the old ways and the new. Its diverse cultural groups must learn to live together peacefully and to respect one another's beliefs and traditions. People of goodwill are determined to meet that challenge and to create a California that has room enough for all.

Chapter Four
Governing California

California government has always produced its fair share of colorful politicians and controversial issues. Often the drama comes from three direct-participation laws: initiative, referendum, and recall. These laws give citizens a chance to shape their own government.

THREE BRANCHES

The basic structure of California government is like that of most other states. It is divided into three branches: executive, legislative, and judicial. Direct participation makes the California electorate into a kind of "fourth branch."

Executive

The governor is chief executive officer of the state, elected for a four-year term. No governor may serve more than two back-to-back terms, for a total of eight years. The governor appoints state, county, and municipal judges—who serve in cities and smaller communities—as well as members of various agencies and commissions. He or she prepares the state budget and submits it to the legislature. The governor can also veto, or reject, measures that the legislature has approved.

California's capitol towers over surrounding Sacramento. The capitol is sometimes referred to as the People's Building, reflecting the state government's mission to serve all Californians.

California has had some interesting and influential governors over the years. Earl Warren served for ten years, before term limits were established, and went on to become the chief justice of the U.S. Supreme Court. Ronald Reagan served eight years. The national attention he gained as governor played an important part in his eventual rise to the presidency.

One California family has had a remarkable impact on the California governorship. Edmund G. "Pat" Brown served from 1959 to 1967. His son, Edmund G. "Jerry" Brown Jr., was also a two-term governor, from 1975 to 1983. Pat's daughter, Kathleen, ran unsuccessfully for the office in 1994.

All the Browns have been liberal Democrats, concerned about social programs and equal rights. The senior Brown improved welfare programs for California's poor and established a master plan for higher education in the state. Jerry Brown created an agency to protect the rights of migrant farmworkers and appointed liberal judges to the bench.

His methods were much different from his father's, though. The younger Brown lived in a modest apartment instead of the governor's mansion, drove a modest car, and generally rejected the pomp and circumstance that usually goes with high office.

In 2003 California became the scene of a political soap opera. With the state facing record debt, residents voted to recall, or remove from office, Governor Gray Davis less than a year after re-electing him to a second term.

After a hotly contested election, actor Arnold Schwarzenegger became the new governor of California. When previous actor/governor Ronald Reagan ran for governor, he had largely retired from his career in show business. Schwarzenegger's campaign, however, competed for media attention with his latest movie, *Terminator 3: Rise of the Machines*.

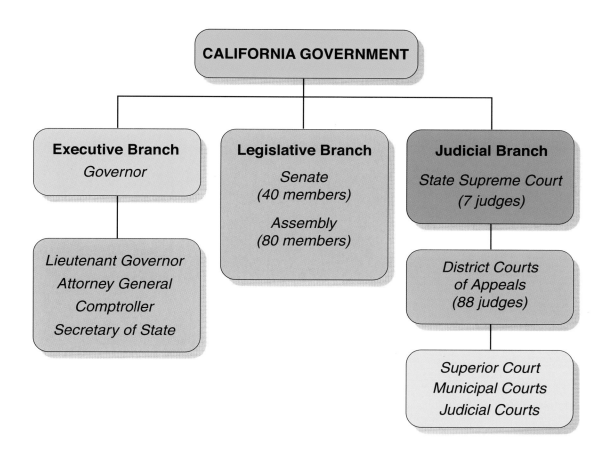

CALIFORNIA GOVERNMENT

Executive Branch
Governor

Lieutenant Governor
Attorney General
Comptroller
Secretary of State

Legislative Branch
Senate
(40 members)

Assembly
(80 members)

Judicial Branch
State Supreme Court
(7 judges)

District Courts
of Appeals
(88 judges)

Superior Court
Municipal Courts
Judicial Courts

Legislative

The legislature is the branch of the state government that creates laws. It is made up of two houses: a forty-member senate and an eighty-member assembly. State senators are elected for four-year terms and are limited to two terms. Assembly members, called representatives, are elected for two years with a maximum of three terms.

For a proposal to become law, it must receive a majority vote in both houses and be signed by the governor. If the governor uses his or her veto power, the legislature can override it if two-thirds of both houses agree.

From world-class bodybuilder to actor to governor, Arnold Schwarzenegger took charge of the state after voters recalled former governor Gray Davis.

For most of its history, California did not have term limits for senators and representatives. Then in 1990, voters approved a term-limit law. Assembly speaker Willie Brown, who had served in the legislature over the course of three decades, challenged the law in the U.S. Supreme Court. In March 1992, the court ruled that the term-limit law was constitutional. Brown left the legislature but not public life. In 1995 he was elected mayor of San Francisco, to the delight of his supporters across the state.

Judicial

California has three types of trial courts: superior, municipal, and justice. Each county has one superior court and a number of municipal and justice courts. The superior court hears felonies, or cases involving major crimes, and civil suits involving more than $15,000. Municipal and justice courts decide the fate of people charged with misdemeanors, or minor crimes, and civil cases concerning sums of less than $15,000.

When someone challenges the ruling of a trial court, one of six district-appeals courts hear the matter. If there is another challenge, the state supreme court is then requested to review the case.

DIRECT LEGISLATION

California has a strong tradition of direct citizen participation in the lawmaking process. Through initiative, referendum, and recall, voters can pass new laws, override those adopted by the legislature, or throw elected officials out of office before their terms expire.

Other states use direct-participation measures but not so widely as California. In the 1990 general election, for example, voters had to decide on twenty-eight different propositions. One of them was the term-limit law that unseated assembly speaker Willie Brown.

Citizens of all ages have a hand in shaping the laws and policies of their state. In May 2003, protestors voiced their criticism of a proposed cut in education spending.

A state as large and as complex as California must have several levels of government in order to function efficiently. California's fifty-eight counties are governed by five-member supervisory boards, chosen in local elections. The candidates running for the posts are not associated with any political parties. A county supervisor is supposed to act more like a business manager than a politician. This means that he or she should be more interested in sound business practices than politics.

California cities are generally run by elected councils and a mayor or professional city manager who sees to the day-to-day operation of city business. In large cities, the mayor is elected to the office and often has great power. In small cities, the position may be less influential. The mayor is simply a council member chosen to chair the meetings and represent the city at ceremonies and various functions. "I'm the guy you yell at when something goes wrong at city hall," said one small-town mayor.

Important California mayors have included Dianne Feinstein of San Francisco, who went on to a seat in the U.S. Senate; Tom Bradley of Los Angeles, one of the first African Americans to head a predominately white city; and Pete Wilson of San Diego, who went on to become the governor of the state.

Tom Bradley was first elected mayor of Los Angeles in 1973. A popular official, he oversaw two decades of economic growth for the city.

CALIFORNIA
BY COUNTY

DEL
NORTE

SISKIYOU

MODOC

HUMBOLDT

TRINITY

SHASTA

LASSEN

TEHAMA

PLUMAS

MENDOCINO

GLENN

BUTTE

SIERRA

LAKE

COLUSA

SUTTER

YUBA

NEVADA

PLACER

SONOMA

YOLO

EL DORADO

NAPA

SACRAMENTO

AMADOR

ALPINE

MARIN

SOLANO

CALAVERAS

CONTRA
COSTA

SAN
JOAQUIN

TUOLUMNE

SAN FRANCISCO

ALAMEDA

MONO

SAN MATEO

STANISLAUS

SANTA
CLARA

MARIPOSA

SANTA CRUZ

MERCED

MADERA

SAN BENITO

FRESNO

MONTEREY

INYO

TULARE

KINGS

SAN LUIS
OBISPO

KERN

SANTA
BARBARA

SAN BERNARDINO

VENTURA

LOS ANGELES

ORANGE

RIVERSIDE

SAN DIEGO

IMPERIAL

LAW AND ORDER, CALIFORNIA STYLE

Law-enforcement agencies in California work hard to keep residents of cities, counties, and the entire state safe. The highway patrol polices the highways, enforcing speed and vehicle-related laws. Every county has a sheriff's department to patrol areas that lie outside of cities. Sheriff's deputies run the county jails and assist at superior-court sessions. Municipal police departments work within city limits.

BATTLING VIOLENT CRIME

In California, like elsewhere, law-enforcement agencies and citizen groups are especially concerned about violent crime. In 1990 California had a rate of 918 violent crimes per 100,000 people—the third highest in the nation. Eleven years later, the state had improved. The rate of violent crimes per 100,000 dropped to 617, making California eighth in the nation instead of third.

The struggle against violent crime has caused many Californians to demand tougher sentencing laws for repeat offenders and to favor the death penalty. Chief Justice Rose Bird of the state supreme court was an outspoken foe of capital punishment. Under her leadership, the court reviewed

California's three-strikes law has divided the state. Some citizens are in favor of stiff penalties for repeat offenders. Others, such as this family, feel their relatives were given unusually long sentences for minor offenses.

sixty-eight death-penalty cases and threw out sixty-four of them. Angry citizens voted her out of office. Under her successor, Justice Malcolm M. Lucas, the court upheld 173 of 203 death sentences.

The voters' next target was repeat offenders. Even the most violent of these criminals often served only a small part of each sentence before being paroled back into the community to possibly commit new crimes. It took a particularly vicious crime to bring the situation to a head.

In October 1993, twelve-year-old Polly Klaas was kidnapped from her home and later murdered. The man who confessed to the killing was a two-time parolee with a lifelong criminal record and a history of violence. He was on parole for kidnapping a woman when he walked into the Klaas home and took Polly.

In the next election, outraged Californians passed a tough new sentencing law. "Three strikes and you're out" closed the revolving door for violent offenders. With three convictions, they went to prison for twenty-five years to life.

CRACKDOWN ON DRUNK DRIVING

Like every other state, California has its share of crimes that are not committed by career criminals. Driving under the influence of alcohol is one of these offenses. Every year, police arrest thousands of drunk drivers. Every year, thousands of other drunk drivers manage to avoid being caught until they cause an accident.

To cope with the problem, California has some of the strictest drunk-driving laws in the nation. A driver is considered to be "under the influence" with a blood-alcohol concentration (BAC) of .08 (one or two drinks). First-time offenders face a fine of $390 to $1,000 and up to six

California's police officers work hard to keep the peace and to ensure the state's citizens are safe.

months in jail. Two convictions within a seven-year period can bring a $1,000 fine and a year in jail.

California does not stop with punishing those who break the rules. Many state and private agencies have programs to stop drunk driving before it starts. Community-service groups offer free rides home on New Year's Eve and other holidays when drinking is usually part of the celebration. On Saturday nights in many country towns, police drive by the lodge halls at closing time. Just the sight of a squad car makes drinkers think twice about driving home.

A clever way to keep people from mixing alcohol and getting behind the wheel is by choosing a designated driver. It has become almost fashionable in trendy California: one person agrees to stay sober and drive everyone else home. To encourage the practice, some restaurants and bars offer a selection of nonalcoholic cocktails for designated drivers.

EDUCATION AND HUMAN SERVICES

California has a vast network of human services: schools and libraries, parks and recreation, health care, welfare, and child-protective agencies. Many of these programs are mandated, or required, by the state but operated by the counties.

Child-abuse prevention is a good example of the ways that California's state government looks out for its youngest residents. By law, a teacher, health-care provider, or other caregiver who suspects that a child has been abused must file a report. County social services handle the investigation.

Private groups such as Parents Anonymous (PA) work to assist social-service agencies. PA is a national organization with headquarters in California. It deals directly with abusive parents, helping them learn new and better ways to discipline their children.

Another major way the state empowers its youth is through the public-school system, which spends $4,608 per year on each of its approximately six million students. A state board of education sets course standards, oversees teacher certification, and is in charge of spending state and federal funds. Local districts are responsible for the day-to-day operation of schools in their communities. They hire teachers and other school staff, maintain buildings, purchase books and supplies, and operate bus services.

In the 1980s and 1990s, California changed the way its schools taught history and social studies. A new multicultural approach includes the contributions of different ethnic and racial groups. Students still learn about the pilgrims who landed at Plymouth Rock, but they also learn about

A ranger teaches these fifth graders about the plants and animals found in one of the state's many parks.

THE CRISIS IN EDUCATION

In September 1995, state superintendent of public instruction Delaine Eastin made an announcement that shocked the people of California: the math and reading reforms of the previous decade had been "a mistake."

State education officials had done away with fundamentals such as phonics, spelling, and basic arithmetic—anything that involved drill and repetition. Instead of memorizing multiplication tables and practicing long division, students were learning "mathematical concepts." Instead of practicing phonics, they learned to read by reading. The idea was to give students literature they would enjoy and let them learn through word recognition.

The bottom line? Too many California students couldn't read, write, or do simple arithmetic. In 1997 a task force began addressing the problem. The committee studied the courses, teacher training, and school funding. The goal was to identify problem areas and create a plan for improvement.

the Native Americans who were there to meet them. They learn about human rights and the dangers of racism.

Though multicultural education has a serious purpose, it also has a lighter side. Some of the study units are as much fun as a role-playing game. At one northern California high school, students studied Native American culture by building an entire village and staging a festival there.

The project affected every class in the school. Native American ideas served as the basis for math, English, reading, history, and social studies projects. Twice a week, the students worked on their village. They built a

In 1998 Governor Pete Wilson signed a new law that dealt with social promotions, the practice of sending all students on to the next grade no matter how they performed in class and on tests. Under the new law, a student's grades and classroom performance had to justify promotion.

In 1999 the state legislature moved from evaluating students to evaluating schools. The Public Schools Accountability Act of 1999 set new standards for schools. The Academic Performance Index (API) measured how well individual schools met those standards. The API used a scale of 200 to 1,000, with 1,000 being the best and 200 the worst.

The first ratings made in 2000 set a "baseline" for each school. When the schools' performances were examined again, more than two-thirds of them had improved their scores. State superintendent of public instruction Delaine Eastin made it clear that the schools still have a lot of work to do. However, the scores "reinforce[d] our belief that we are on the right path."

tule house, a bark lodge, and a small tepee. When the work was done, they threw a party for the whole community, with Native American dancers and Native American foods.

These girls are hard at their lessons, practicing their flutes at a San Mateo music camp.

Chapter Five

Making a Living

California's economy is made up of many facets, with agriculture, aerospace, electronics, entertainment, high technology, and manufacturing all contributing to the mix. These industries support thousands of retail and service businesses, from fast-food restaurants and stores to gas stations, supermarkets, and dog groomers. State and local government also helps to create jobs in utilities, highway maintenance, law enforcement, health care, and education.

DIRECT LEGISLATION AND THE ECONOMY

Through the initiative process, California voters can shape the state budget both directly and indirectly. For example, Proposition 98 affected the budget directly. This 1988 initiative required that the state spend 40 percent of its money on public schools and junior colleges.

The "three strikes" law that imposed lengthy prison sentences for repeat offenders had nothing to do with money. However, it had a great deal to do with budgeting. It costs more than a half-million dollars to keep one offender in prison for twenty-five years. In addition,

A local grower proudly displays the tomatoes and other fruits and vegetables he has raised.

these long-term inmates become a burden on California's already over-crowded prison system. Building new prisons and expanding existing ones costs millions of dollars as well.

Perhaps the best-known of all California economic measures was Proposition 13. This response to ever-higher taxes grew out of rising property values in the 1970s. In less than ten years, the value of a single-family home had gone up 43 percent. Higher property values meant higher property taxes. Many Californians had to give up their homes because they could not afford to pay the taxes.

Proposition 13 limited property taxes to 1 percent of assessed value. That means that taxes on a house valued at $50,000 could not be more than $500 per year. This measure not only altered California's tax structure, but inspired other states to adopt similar changes.

2005 GROSS STATE PRODUCT: $1.4 TRILLION

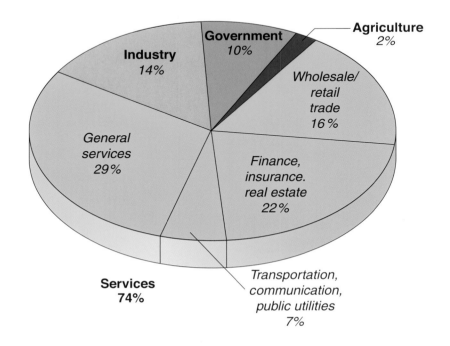

Government 10%

Agriculture 2%

Industry 14%

Wholesale/ retail trade 16%

General services 29%

Finance, insurance. real estate 22%

Services 74%

Transportation, communication, public utilities 7%

STEADY GROWTH

At the beginning of the 1980s, California had the largest commercial bank in the country, the top six savings and loans, the biggest supermarket chain, and the most television and movie producers in the world. Silicon Valley was leading the way in the home-computer revolution. The state's economy was on more than steady footing.

DOWN AND OUT IN THE NINETIES

By the beginning of the 1990s, cracks had appeared in California's economy. Real estate prices soared so high that many families would never be able to buy their own home. A scandal in the savings-and-loan industry drained millions from the economy. Massive closures of military bases threw thousands of people out of work. Even Silicon Valley slowed its rate of growth.

For the first time in history, large numbers of people began leaving California for other locations. Between 1991 and 1994, the state lost about one million residents.

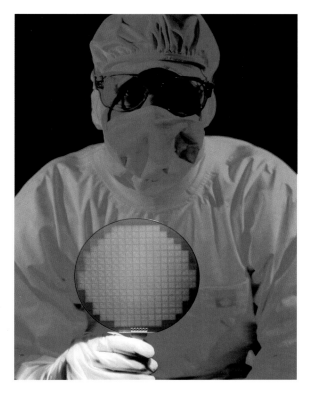

California has long been a technology leader. New developments and discoveries are being made in the state's laboratories and research centers.

THE APPLE MAN

In the 1970s, computers were huge machines that took up too much floor space and strained the budgets of even the largest companies. A young man from the northern California community of Los Altos wanted to change all that.

Steve Jobs, the adopted son of Paul and Clara Jobs, was something of a loner. He did not work well in groups or know how to make small talk. His mind was quick, creative, and restless. At Reed College in Oregon, he experimented with meditation and Eastern philosophy. That took him to India, where he backpacked across the country in search of a guru, a spiritual teacher who could show him the secrets of life.

By 1975 he was helping his friend Steve Wozniak create a revolutionary computer circuit board. Unlike the giant machines in use at the time, Wozniak's board was small, lightweight, and not too expensive to produce. Steve Jobs was certain he could find a market for it.

The partners worked in Jobs's garage, making boards to sell to computer manufacturers. Wozniak built the boards, and Jobs tried to sell them. When his

People who stayed faced hardship. Twenty-five-year-old Arturo Garcia worked seven days a week at three different jobs just to stay afloat. Most nights, he got only four hours of sleep. "Sometimes it takes . . . an hour to wake me up. I'm always saying, 'Just five more minutes, just five more minutes.'"

Many experts thought quality-of-life issues drove people away. They said that traffic congestion, air pollution, street violence, and earthquakes had finally caught up with a state many once viewed as paradise. A study by very first sales call produced an order for fifty units, he got an idea. Why stop with circuit boards? Why not build a whole computer?

With that question, the Apple personal computer was born. Wozniak engineered the circuitry, while Jobs handled design and promotion. He wanted to create a whole new kind of computer: one that was trim, easy to move, and simple to operate. To describe what he meant, he coined the term *user-friendly*.

When Apple's first personal computer hit the market in 1977, the company kept its cash receipts in a desk drawer. Three years later, it had total sales of $139 million. In the best California tradition, Steve Jobs became a multimillionaire before he turned thirty. He also became one of those rags-to-riches success stories that have always delighted Californians and people everywhere.

economists at the Federal Reserve Bank in San Francisco showed otherwise. People moved away to find jobs, not to escape the California lifestyle.

California-born Brian Austin is typical of those who left. A skilled aircraft mechanic in his midtwenties, Austin could not find a job anywhere in the state. He ended up taking an entry-level position with a firm in Texas. "They came to California to recruit people like me," he said. "They offered a good salary and a bonus . . . even paid my moving expenses."

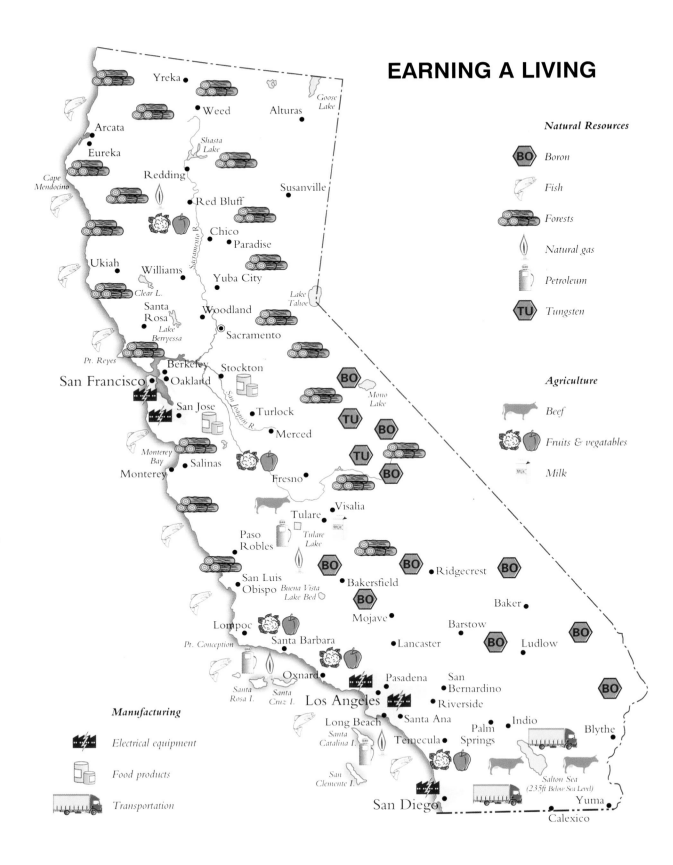

EARNING A LIVING

Natural Resources

BO Boron

Fish

Forests

Natural gas

Petroleum

TU Tungsten

Agriculture

Beef

Fruits & vegatables

Milk

Manufacturing

Electrical equipment

Food products

Transportation

Yreka
Weed
Alturas
Goose Lake
Arcata
Shasta Lake
Eureka
Cape Mendocino
Redding
Red Bluff
Susanville
Chico
Paradise
Ukiah
Williams
Yuba City
Lake Tahoe
Santa Rosa
Clear L.
Woodland
Lake Berryessa
Sacramento
Pt. Reyes
Berkeley
Stockton
San Francisco
Oakland
BO
San Jose
Mono Lake
Turlock
TU
Merced
BO
Monterey Bay
TU
Salinas
Monterey
Fresno
BO
Tulare
Visalia
Paso Robles
Tulare Lake
Pt. Conception
San Luis Obispo
Buena Vista Lake Bed
BO
Bakersfield
Ridgecrest
BO
Baker
Mojave
Barstow
BO
Lompoc
Santa Barbara
Lancaster
BO Ludlow
Santa Rosa I.
Santa Cruz I.
Oxnard
Pasadena
San Bernardino
BO
Los Angeles
Riverside
Long Beach
Santa Ana
Indio
Santa Catalina I.
Temecula
Palm Springs
Blythe
San Clemente I.
Salton Sea (235ft Below Sea Level)
San Diego
Yuma
Calexico
Sacramento R.
San Joaquin R.

Like many who left during the downturn, Brian Austin did not mean to leave California permanently. It just worked out that way. "Living expenses were so much less, especially housing," he explained. "Then I met my wife, and I guess we've just settled in. I don't think I'll ever live in California again . . . just come back for visits."

In the mid-1990s, California began getting back some of its old steam. The economy survived the savings-and-loan scandals. Business groups set to work converting military bases for other uses. More jobs were created. Though many problems remained, people told each other that the worst was over. They were right.

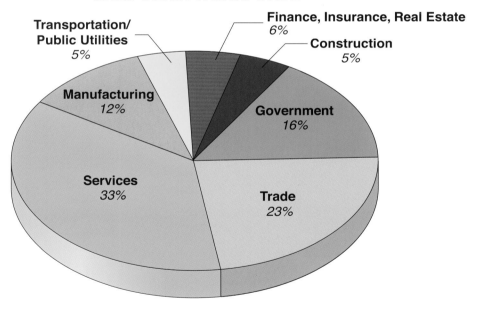

CALIFORNIA WORKFORCE

Transportation/Public Utilities 5%

Finance, Insurance, Real Estate 6%

Construction 5%

Manufacturing 12%

Government 16%

Services 33%

Trade 23%

The mid-1990s also saw increased trade with Canada and Mexico because of the North American Free Trade Agreement (NAFTA). Silicon Valley blossomed with free-spending dot-coms, ready to put California on the cutting edge of the Information Age.

CALIFORNIA AND NAFTA

On December 8, 1993, President Bill Clinton signed the North American Free Trade Agreement. The United States, Mexico, and Canada removed barriers such as import taxes to allow the free flow of goods and services across borders.

A container ship glides under the Golden Gate Bridge and enters San Francisco Bay.

California felt the impact of NAFTA almost immediately. Some companies moved to Mexico to take advantage of lower costs of facilities, labor, and other essentials. For example, Stanley Door Systems, which makes door hardware, moved from San Dimas, California, to Mexico. Eighty jobs went with it. International Rectifiers, assemblers of semiconductors or memory chips, took their 130 jobs to Mexico.

Many California leaders believe that these losses are more than offset by the gains. In NAFTA's first seven years, exports from California to Canada and Mexico increased by $7.4 billion and $12.5 billion, respectively. This growth in exports produced 239,000 new jobs.

DOT-COMS AND DEFICITS

By the late 1990s, Silicon Valley dot-com companies were riding a wave of success. Nobody seemed to care about profits. The e-businesses, as they are also often called, considered themselves pioneers. They expected to lose money at first, but they believed that profits would come in time. Investors seemed to agree with them. Dot-com stock prices soared as investors bought themselves pieces of the California high-tech dream. In 2000 that dream ended.

Stock prices plunged. Dozens of dot-coms went out of business. Workers lost jobs, and investors lost money. The rest of the high-tech industry suffered in the fallout. For example, memory-chip-maker Intel saw its earnings drop by 70 percent, from $10.5 billion in 2000 to $3.6 billion in 2001.

Plunging profits for companies meant less tax money for the state. California found itself with a budget it could no longer afford. While the economy was staggering from this blow, an energy crisis hit the state. In the winter of 2001, power companies could not generate enough elec-

The state's economy has seen its share of shaky times. These out-of-work Californians gathered in Sunnyvale in order to meet with recruiters and find new jobs.

tricity to keep up with demand. Creating rolling blackouts and buying power from outside sources at high prices became the best solution.

These crises hit hard. California found itself with a budget deficit of $38 billion. That is more than the entire budget of most other states and several small countries as well. Californians are known for setting trends and taking chances. They are not easily shocked. However, the sheer size of this deficit not only shocked but angered them as well.

The deficit was a major reason for the recall election of 2003, in which Californians voted Gray Davis out of office and chose Arnold Schwarzenegger to take his place. With that change in place, they went back to doing what they have always done: weathering the ups and downs of the world's fifth-largest economy.

Chapter Six

Out and About in California

Touring California is a major undertaking; there is so much to see and do in the Golden State. From the mission trail of the Spanish padres to sprawling cities, quaint gold-rush towns, and towering redwood forests, California is a place of many wonders. Here are some of the highlights in a quick tour.

EL CAMINO REAL

A good place to start a tour of California is where the Spanish explorers began in 1769: at San Diego, just across the present Mexican border. It was there that Father Junípero Serra founded San Diego de Alcalá, the first of a chain of twenty-one missions that would reach to Sonoma in the northern part of the state. Modern Highway 101 follows a nearly identical route.

The missions were spaced a day's journey apart, and each controlled vast areas of surrounding land. Mission Santa Barbara, for example, had 122,000 acres. The missions themselves were laid out in the Spanish manner, with

Early evening descends on the bell tower of the Santa Barbara Mission church.

buildings surrounding a large central courtyard. In addition to a chapel, there were workshops, living and dining quarters, a library, and an infirmary, or medical office.

Buildings were made of adobe (sun-baked bricks of mud and straw) covered with whitewashed plaster. Red-tiled roofs made a striking contrast. Most of the missions have been restored, at least in part. Some still function as churches. Mission San Buenaventura is home to an active parish. Its midnight Mass on Christmas Eve draws Catholics and non-Catholics alike to the sanctuary.

SAN DIEGO AND THE SOUTH COUNTIES

San Diego is a city of contrasts. It is a metropolitan center, with high-rise buildings and crowded freeways. It is also a fun-loving beach town, with yacht harbors, quaint seafood restaurants, and mile after mile of glorious beaches.

The San Diego Zoo occupies 100 acres of Balboa Park. The animals live in display areas that resemble their natural habitats. Instead of cages, there are desert, tundra, grassland, and tropical rain forest. There is also a zoo nursery, where motherless animals are raised by human caretakers.

Downtown San Diego features the beautifully restored Gaslamp Quarter, which is often called the New Orleans of the West. This approximately sixteen-block area is more than a tourist attraction; it is like a living history museum. It has authentic buildings, fixtures, and furnishings and an atmosphere of days gone by. There are shops, art galleries, and sidewalk cafés.

THE DESERT

Less than 150 miles from the ocean breezes and salt air of San Diego, Palm Springs is the glamour capital of the southern desert. Celebrities

A layer of glass separates a family from a hippopotamus swimming in one of the tanks at the San Diego Zoo.

such as Frank Sinatra, Bob Hope, and Elvis Presley have vacationed there, along with at least five presidents—Eisenhower, Kennedy, Johnson, Nixon, and Ford. An aerial tramway runs from town to the Mount San Jacinto wilderness. The tram is the world's largest and longest, 2.5 miles from station to station, with cars that hold up to eighty passengers.

Joshua Tree National Monument preserves a strange and fascinating plant. The Joshua tree is actually a giant cactus, which can grow up to 50 feet tall and live for several hundred years. A young Joshua tree begins its life as

TEN LARGEST CITIES

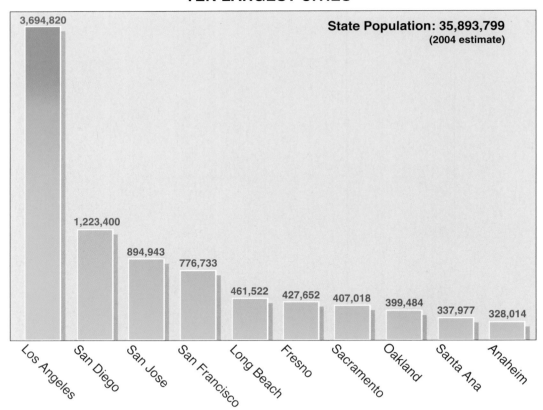

State Population: 35,893,799
(2004 estimate)

Los Angeles	3,694,820
San Diego	1,223,400
San Jose	894,943
San Francisco	776,733
Long Beach	461,522
Fresno	427,652
Sacramento	407,018
Oakland	399,484
Santa Ana	337,977
Anaheim	328,014

a fleshy stalk, thrusting upward from the ground. Limbs form as it grows, and the whole plant bends and twists itself into strange shapes. At sundown the sight of Joshua trees against an orange desert sky is eerie and strangely beautiful.

Farther north in the Mojave Desert are towns with interesting names such as Twentynine Palms and Apple Valley. Once sparsely populated, these desert areas have become popular resorts. In the 1980s, towns such as Victorville and Hesperia grew rapidly as people moved to the desert for affordable housing and cleaner air.

West of the deserts, in the Orange County city of Anaheim, lies what is perhaps California's most famous attraction: Disneyland. The park was born in the imagination of Walt Disney and has drawn millions of visitors since its opening in 1955. From the soda and gift shops of Main Street, U.S.A., to an Old West frontier town and a spaceship bound for strange planets, Disneyland offers visitors a chance to live out their fantasies.

A crescent moon lights up the otherwise dark skies over Joshua Tree National Monument.

Los Angeles is a sprawling city that fans out into suburb after suburb. Among its many points of interest are fabled places such as Hollywood, Beverly Hills, and Westwood. Westwood is a college town, home to the University of California, Los Angeles (UCLA). Its broad streets are lined with cafés, coffeehouses, and bookstores that cater to the students living there.

A PLACE THAT NEVER WAS

Author Helen Hunt Jackson set her 1884 novel, *Ramona*, in the deserts of Riverside County, near the little town of Hemet. She wrote the book to protest the United States's mistreatment of Native Americans, but nobody noticed the social commentary. Readers got caught up in the story of Ramona Ortegna, adopted daughter of a Spanish nobleman. Her forbidden love for the Indian Alesandro ended in tragedy.

The book was so popular that people began coming to see the place where Ramona and Alesandro were supposed to have been married, the place where he was killed, and the place where she prepared to flee to Mexico with their child in her arms.

Nobody seemed to care that Ramona was a fictional character. Her myth inspired three movies, one sentimental song, and an annual outdoor pageant. Each year the citizens of Hemet stage the story, with appropriate costumes and ceremony. People come from long distances to see it and maybe shed a tear for California's very own star-crossed lovers.

Two palm trees frame part of downtown Los Angeles. Mount Baldy pokes up, containing the sprawling city beyond.

Beverly Hills is known for movie-star mansions and the pricey shopping along Rodeo Drive. Both have been featured in countless movies and television shows. Hollywood itself is no longer the movie capital of California, since most of the studios have moved into outlying areas. But television and recording companies still have offices there, and stars still leave their marks in the form of their footprints and handprints in the concrete slabs outside Mann's Chinese Theater.

Griffith Park is the largest city park in California, with approximately 4,100 acres. In addition to riding trails and picnic areas, it includes a six-thousand-seat Greek theater, a planetarium, and an observatory. The Griffith Park Zoo houses animals from all over the world in comfortable, naturalistic settings.

Los Angeles has many fine cultural facilities, including the center for the performing arts which contains a symphony hall, a large auditorium, and a small theater for experimental drama. The Los Angeles County Museum of Art is the largest art museum west of the Mississippi River, with more than 250,000 pieces in its permanent collection.

One of the best-known sites in the area is the Hollywood Bowl. This natural amphitheater has a stage backed by a shell. The Hollywood Bowl is famous for its summer program Symphonies under the Stars.

THE CENTRAL COAST AND THE BAY AREA

Moving up the coast, the traveler meets up with a four-county area of beautiful beaches and pleasant seaside towns. North of San Luis Obispo is one of California's most famous landmarks: San Simeon, sometimes called Hearst Castle. Built by multimillionaire William Randolph Hearst, the castle is now a state monument.

The house and grounds cover 127 acres, including elaborate pools, gardens, terraces, and guest houses. There is even a private zoo. The main house contains some of the world's great art treasures, along with priceless artifacts. There are ceilings from medieval monasteries, fireplaces from Gothic castles, statues from Egyptian temples, and tapestries from Byzantine churches.

San Francisco is a world-class city with landmarks and legends enough for anyone. It marches over the hills between the Pacific Ocean and San Francisco Bay. The famous

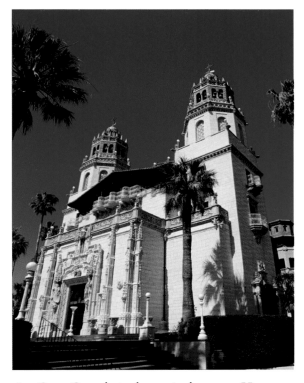

La Casa Grande is the main house at Hearst Castle in San Simeon.

Golden Gate Bridge spans the entrance to the bay, connecting San Francisco to Marin County. The bridge is 4,200 feet long, with towers standing 746 feet high.

The skyline of "the City," as some San Franciscans call their home, is one of the most beautiful—and recognizable—in the world. It has appeared in so many movies and television shows that millions recognize its steep hills and Victorian row houses on sight.

Across the bay from San Francisco, Oakland and Berkeley are major cities in their own right. Berkeley is home to a University of California

This view from the top of the south tower of San Francisco's Golden Gate Bridge shows a city wrapped in fog.

(UC) campus, as well as a number of smaller private colleges. One section near the UC campus has so many seminaries, or centers for religious training, that the locals call it Holy Hill. Oakland marks the western end of the transcontinental railway and is a major port and shipbuilding center as well.

WINE COUNTRY

The center of California's wine country is Napa Valley, where the weather and the soil are perfect for vineyards. Wineries dot the landscape, many of them made of stone and covered with ivy. In the town of Calistoga, hot mineral springs draw people to fashionable spas.

The wine country also includes Sonoma, Mendocino, and Lake counties, all of which have vineyards and wineries of their own. Sonoma County is the site of the Luther Burbank Center, a performing-arts facility in the city of Santa Rosa. The center was named for the Sonoma County naturalist whose studies of plant genetics led to the creation of several dozen new species. Mendocino County is noted for its redwood trees and seaports that look like New England fishing villages.

Lake County produces wine, but its real claim to fame is Clear Lake, which is more than two million years old. Some people say that the ancient lake is showing its age. The annual algae blooms, or rapid growths, give the lake water a greenish cast and a strong odor. This annoys boaters and fishermen but does little actual damage. Because the bloom rises from the deep bottom, the lake literally seems to turn inside out. Local citizens have dubbed algae season, "As the Lake Turns," a play on the title of a popular daytime TV drama, *As the World Turns*.

Row upon row of grapes grow in Napa Valley, one of the state's main wine-making regions.

GOLD COUNTRY

In the foothills of the Sierra Nevada, a number of quiet historic towns recall the history of the gold rush. Sonora, Columbia, and Jamestown cluster in Tuolumne County near the center of the mother lode, or main deposit. This 100-mile-long network of veins is made up of gold-bearing quartz.

PLACES TO SEE

Yreka

Weed

Alturas

Goose Lake

Arcata

Eureka

Shasta Lake

Cape Mendocino

Redding

Lassen Volcanic NP

Susanville

Red Bluff

Sacramento R.

Chico

Paradise

Ukiah

Williams

Yuba City

Lake Tahoe

Clear L.

Santa Rosa

Woodland

Lake Berryessa

Sacramento

Pt. Reyes

Berkeley

Stockton

Yosemite

San Francisco

Oakland

Mono Lake

San Jose

Modesto

Turlock

San Joaquin R.

Merced

Monterey Bay

Salinas

Monterey

Fresno

Visalia

Tulare

Porterville

Paso Robles

Tulare Lake

Bakersfield

Ridgecrest

San Luis Obispo

Buena Vista Lake Bed

Mojave Desert

Baker

Santa Maria

Mojave

Barstow

Lompoc

Pt. Conception

Santa Barbara

Lancaster

Ludlow

Santa Barbara Channel

Mojave Desert

Beverly Hills

Santa Rosa I.

Santa Cruz I.

Oxnard

Los Angeles

RODEO DRIVE

Griffith Park

Joshua Tree National Monument

Blythe

Palm Springs

The Los Angeles County Museum of Art

Santa Catalina I.

Gulf of Santa Catalina

San Diego

Salton Sea (235ft Below Sea Level)

Disneyland

San Clemente I.

San Diego Zoo

Yuma

Back in the days of the forty-niners, Sonora was known as the most violent and lawless town in all of gold country. Prospector William Perkins kept a kind of body count in his journal. He recorded four killings in the third week of June 1850 and six more in the second week of July.

Present-day Sonora is a peaceful, gracious town, beautifully restored to keep its nineteenth-century charm. Victorian houses look as fresh as the day they were built, and the steeple of the wooden church rises over the town's main street. Antique shops, mining supply stores, and delightful hole-in-the-wall bookstores dot the business district.

In Columbia twelve square blocks of the old town have been designated a state historic park. Restored buildings include a Wells Fargo office, a Masonic temple, a firehouse, a schoolhouse, and a newspaper office, along with the saloons and stores that once served the miners' daily needs. The main street of the restored area is closed to automobiles; only horse-drawn vehicles may enter.

Jamestown sits over the exact center of the mother lode. In the early 1990s, it was the scene of great excitement when somebody unearthed a 60-pound nugget of pure gold. The unexpected discovery had quite a number of people dreaming about a second gold rush. Unfortunately, the dream did not last for long; the Super Nugget turned out to be an isolated find, not the beginning of a new strike.

YOSEMITE

Naturalist John Muir was so moved by the Sierra Nevada that he spoke of them in almost religious terms: "Climb the mountains and get their good tidings. Nature's peace will flow into you as sunshine flows into trees. The winds will blow their freshness into you and the storms their energies while cares will drop off like autumn leaves."

Visitors to California's gold country can try their hands at panning, a technique early miners used in their search for gold. They swished gravel, loose dirt, and a little water in a shallow pan to try and find the valuable ore.

Yosemite National Park is a protected area so it can be enjoyed by countless generations to come.

Of all the magnificent territory in the Sierras, Muir loved Yosemite the most. He was determined to protect this scenic wildland from the builders, businesspeople, treasure hunters, and settlers who would bend it to their own use.

Thanks largely to his efforts, Yosemite became a national park in 1890. Its 761,236 acres include towering mountains and a valley carved by prehistoric glaciers. The wilderness seems like a place out of time, with crystal waterfalls spilling over jagged cliffs, rock formations taking fantastical shapes, and groves of giant sequoias towering over the land. Some of those sequoias are more than 2,700 years old.

The natural splendor of Yosemite makes a fitting end to a tour of California, having come, in a sense, full circle from the forty-niners who risked everything to cross the mighty Sierra Nevada to modern tourists who go there to surround themselves with nature.

In a state known for setting trends and adapting to change, Yosemite is a reminder of other, more permanent values. The mountains, the glacial valley, and the ancient trees are as much a part of the California lifestyle as movie studios and computer companies. John Muir would have loved that.

THE FLAG: *The flag was officially adopted in 1911. It shows a grizzly bear on a green patch, a single red star against a white background, and the words* California Republic. *A red strip is at the bottom of the flag. It is modeled after the bear flag flown by American settlers when they revolted against Mexico in 1846.*

THE SEAL: *Adopted in 1849, the seal shows a grizzly bear representing California. Minerva, Roman goddess of wisdom, stands next to it. A sheaf of wheat and grape clusters stand for agriculture, and a miner with a pick symbolizes the state's rich mineral resources and mining history. In the background, ships represent commerce; the mountains are the Sierra Nevada. The state motto appears at the top of the seal.*

State Survey

Statehood: September 9, 1850

Origin of Name: Named by Spanish explorers who sailed along the coast in the 1500s, the origin of the name is not clear. *Las Sergas de Esplandian,* a popular Spanish tale published in the early 1500s, told of a fabulous island ruled by a queen named Calafia. Another possibility is that the name was derived from the Spanish words *caliente fornalla,* meaning "hot furnace."

Nickname: The Golden State

Capital: Sacramento

Motto: Eureka (from Greek *heureka,* meaning "I have found it")

Bird: California quail

Animal: California grizzly bear

Fish: California golden trout

Flower: California poppy

Tree: California redwood

Colors: Blue and gold

Gem: Benitoite

California quail

I LOVE YOU, CALIFORNIA

This song was sung in 1914 aboard the first ship to sail through the Panama Canal on its way to California. It was not adopted as the official state song until 1951.

Music by A.F. Frankenstein

Words by F.B. Silverwood

Stone: Serpentine

Fossil: Saber-toothed cat

Insect: California dogface butterfly

Marine Mammal: California gray whale

Reptile: California desert tortoise

GEOGRAPHY

Highest Point: Mount Whitney, 14,495 feet

Lowest Point: Death Valley, 282 feet below sea level

Area: 163,707 square miles

Greatest Distance North to South: 770 miles

Greatest Distance East to West: 250 miles

Bordering States: Oregon to the north, Nevada and Arizona to the east; Mexico lies to the south

Hottest Recorded Temperature: 134° F in Death Valley on July 10, 1913

Coldest Recorded Temperature: -45° F at Boca, near Truckee, on January 20, 1937

Average Annual Rainfall: 22 inches

Major Rivers: Sacramento, San Joaquin, Colorado, Klamath, Russian, Stanislaus, Tuolumne, Merced, Trinity, Eel

Major Lakes: Tahoe, Salton Sea, Clear, Goose, Eagle, Mono

Trees: cedar, fir, hemlock, giant sequoia, ponderosa pine, California redwood, oak, spruce, maple, Monterey pine, Monterey cypress, aspen, eucalyptus, palm

Wild Plants: lupine, viola, California poppy, cactus, desert poppy, Joshua tree, burroweed, creosote bush, indigo bush, desert evening primrose, sand verbena, chaparral, beardtongue, fiddle-neck, fireweed, Washington lily, myrtle, flowering dogwood

Animals: coyote, lizard, rattlesnake, beaver, deer, cougar, fox, mink, muskrat, hare, wildcat, wild burro, bighorn sheep, wolverine, mountain sheep, pronghorn antelope, elk, bear, desert tortoise, horned toad, kangaroo rat, seal, sea lion, otter, dolphin

Birds: goose, grouse, mourning dove, quail, wild turkey, junco, California thrasher, California condor, hermit thrush, mountain bluebird, wood duck, mallard duck, spotted owl, pelican, tern, gull

Fish and Sea Creatures: black bass, striped bass, salmon, trout, abalone, clam, crab, shrimp, lobster, oyster, scallop, perch, tuna, shark, halibut, marlin, sea bass, red snapper

Northern elephant seals

Endangered Animals: California condor, Point Arena mountain beaver, Pacific pocket mouse, salt-marsh harvest mouse, San Joaquin kit fox, Fresno kangaroo rat, giant kangaroo rat, California brown pelican, California clapper rail, light-footed clapper rail, Yuma clapper rail, San Clemente loggerhead shrike, bald eagle, blunt-nosed leopard lizard, bonytail, Lost River sucker, longhorn fairy shrimp, lotis blue butterfly, Palos Verdes blue butterfly

Endangered Plants: Bakersfield cactus, beach layia, Contra Costa wall-flower, California jewelflower, California Orcutt grass, Eureka Dunes evening primrose, Eureka Valley dune grass, large-flowered fiddle-neck, San Francisco popcorn flower, marsh sandwort, Monterey gilia, Orcutt's spineflower, San Clemente Island woodland star, San Clemente Island bush mallow, San Clemente Island larkspur, San Diego button-celery, San Joaquin woollythreads, slender-horned spineflower, Sonoma sunshine, Tidestrom's lupine, Truckee barberry

TIMELINE

California History

1542 Juan Rodríguez Cabrillo explores California coast

1579 Francis Drake lands on coast, claims land for England

1602 Sebastián Vizcaíno surveys Monterey Bay as a site for a Spanish colony

1769 Spain's first permanent mission established at site of present-day San Diego

1775 Monterey becomes the capital

1776 Spanish settlers from Mexico reach site of present-day San Francisco

1810 Mexican rebellion against Spain begins

1812 Russian fur traders establish Fort Ross north of San Francisco

1816 Thomas Doak becomes the first American settler in California

1821 Spain grants independence to Mexico

1822 California becomes part of Mexico

1826 Jedediah Smith completes the first overland trip by an American to California

1831–1836 California revolts against Mexico

1841 The first American wagon train arrives in California

1842 John C. Frémont leads a U.S. government expedition into California

1846 U.S. settlers in California protest Mexican rule and raise the bear flag in the Bear Flag Revolt

1848 Mexico cedes California and much of the Southwest to the United States in the Treaty of Guadalupe Hidalgo

1848 Gold is discovered at Sutter's Mill

1849 The gold rush begins

1850 California becomes the thirty-first state

1850 James Beckwourth discovers the Sierra Nevada pass

1861 First transcontinental telegraph line is connected

1869 Transcontinental railroad is completed, linking California to East Coast

1887 Real estate and population boom in southern California

1890 Yosemite Park is established

1906 Earthquake and fire destroy much of San Francisco

1911 The first film is shot in Hollywood

1930 Dust Bowl refugees from the Midwest begin moving to California

1932 Olympic Games are held in Los Angeles

1937 Golden Gate Bridge opens

1941 United States enters World War II

1942 Japanese Americans are relocated to internment camps

1945 World War II ends; United Nations is founded in San Francisco

1955 Disneyland opens in Anaheim

1959–1967 Edmund G. "Pat" Brown Sr. serves as governor

1962 Cesar Chavez founds the National Farm Workers Association (becomes United Farm Workers in 1966)

1964 California becomes the nation's most populous state

1966–1974 Ronald Reagan serves as governor

1975–1983 Edmund G. "Jerry" Brown Jr. serves as governor

1978 State voters approve Proposition 13, a state constitutional amendment cutting property taxes by $7 billion

1984 Olympic Games are held in Los Angeles

1989 Earthquake in the San Francisco Bay area

1994 Earthquake in Los Angeles

2003 Arnold Schwarzenegger is elected governor

ECONOMY

Natural Resources: petroleum, natural gas, sand, gravel, stone, boron, tungsten, clay, oil, fish, lumber

Agricultural Products: milk, beef cattle, greenhouse and nursery products, cotton, almonds, grapes, hay, tomatoes

Manufacturing: transportation equipment, electrical equipment, electronic components, computers, military communication equipment, food products, machinery

The entertainment industry

Business and Trade: entertainment, tourism, wholesale and retail trade, finance, insurance, real estate, transportation, communication

Pasadena is the site of the annual New Year's Day Tournament of Roses. The parade, with its exquisite flower-decorated floats, has been held since 1890. Since 1946 the Rose Bowl college football game has pitted the Pacific Coast Conference champion against the Big Ten champion.

Chinese New Year is celebrated in either January or February during a week of festivities in San Francisco. The grand finale is the Golden Dragon Parade through Chinatown.

Chinese New Year

Held in February or March, Snowfest Lake Tahoe is the biggest winter carnival in the West, with skiing, fireworks, parades, and live music.

The Cherry Blossom Festival, held in San Francisco's Japantown in April, features exhibits and a parade.

May Carnival in San Francisco is a multiethnic parade. It includes dancers and samba music, much like *Carnaval* in Brazil.

The Bay-to-Breakers 7.5-mile footrace in May in San Francisco draws 100,000 runners, walkers, and roller skaters, many in outrageous costumes.

As part of the Calaveras County Fair, the town of Angels Camp holds its Jumping Frog Jubilee each May. "The Celebrated Jumping Frog of Calaveras County" was Mark Twain's first published success.

Graffiti U.S.A., held in Modesto in the middle of June, celebrates the 1950s (as seen in the movie *American Graffiti*). It features a street fair with 1950s music, arts and crafts, a car show, and a classic car "cruise" downtown.

Celebrate the summer solstice in Santa Barbara with the Summer Solstice Parade and its giant puppets, weird floats and costumes, and a street fair.

The California Rodeo, one of the largest in the nation, has been held in Salinas since 1911. It is held for four days usually on and around the third weekend of July.

The California State Fair, held in August and early September in the Sacramento area, is a chance to hear top-name singers, watch grape-stomping and pie-eating contests, or view the state's produce and livestock.

The San Francisco Blues Festival is the nation's oldest. Presented in September, it features artists performing outdoors, overlooking the bay and the Golden Gate Bridge.

Thousands of kilted Scots come to Santa Rosa each August or September for the Scottish Gathering and Games. Competitions include putting and throwing the stone and caber tossing. (A caber is a large pole.) There's plenty of bagpipe music and food.

Held in November, the Doo Dah Parade is a spoof of the annual Rose Bowl Parade also held in the city of Pasadena.

The Great Dickens Christmas Fair in San Francisco re-creates the Victorian period with costumes, food, music, and dancing in November.

Celebrating Christmas at Yosemite is a great tradition. A three-hour, seven-course medieval-style meal includes food, music, and song. The Lord of Misrule and his pet bear offer amusing antics.

Ansel Adams (1902–1984), born in San Francisco, was one of the nation's foremost photographic artists. He was noted for his black-and-white photos of Yosemite National Park and other wilderness areas.

Gene Autry (1907–1998), born in Texas, starred in more than eighty Westerns, wrote more than 250 songs, and starred in a television series. He was known as the Singing Cowboy. He also owned television and radio stations in California, as well as a share of baseball's California Angels.

Barbara Boxer (1940–   ), born in Brooklyn, New York, spent ten years as a California representative to Congress before being elected senator in 1992. She has worked to further the rights of women and reduce military spending.

Ray Bradbury (1920–   ), a writer of science-fiction novels and short stories, has been a longtime resident of Los Angeles. His many works include *The Martian Chronicles* and *Fahrenheit 451*, about a society in the future that forbids people to own or read books.

Luther Burbank (1849–1926), born in Massachusetts, spent most of his life in California. He moved to Santa Rosa in 1875, where he became a leading horticulturist. He developed new species and variants of many fruits, flowers, and vegetables, including the potato, the tomato, corn, and peas.

Barbara Boxer

Edgar Rice Burroughs (1875–1950), born in Chicago, lived just north of Los Angeles on an estate he named Tarzana after his famous fictional character, Tarzan. A nearby town now bears the name Tarzana. Burroughs wrote a series of novels, beginning with *Tarzan of the Apes*, about a boy raised by apes in an African jungle.

Cecil B. De Mille (1881–1959) was a pioneer movie director and producer. His epic films, often dealing with biblical or historical subjects, include *The Ten Commandments* in 1923 and a remake in 1956.

Joan Didion (1934–) wrote *Run River,* a novel about her native Sacramento Valley, as well as many other novels, including *Play It as It Lays* and *A Book of Common Prayer.* She has also written essays and film scripts.

Walt Disney (1901–1966) was born in Chicago and moved to Hollywood as a young man. In 1928 he created Mickey Mouse. By 1940 he had established his own studio and developed full-length cartoons, including *Fantasia, Pinocchio,* and *Snow White and the Seven Dwarfs.* He also developed Disneyland in Anaheim in Orange County.

Isadora Duncan (1877–1927) grew up in San Francisco before becoming an actor and dancer in New York, then London and Athens. She was a great influence on modern dance, rebelling against formal classical ballet and using dance as an individual form of expression. She lived abroad most of her career and established dance schools for children in France, Germany, and Russia.

Dianne Feinstein (1933–   ) was the first woman to become a senator from California. She was also the first woman to become mayor of San Francisco. Crime prevention, environmental preservation, and education have been key issues for this Democrat.

Danny Glover (1947–   ), an actor, was born and raised in San Francisco. He has starred in many movies, including *Places in the Heart, The Color Purple,* and the *Lethal Weapon* series.

Samuel Goldwyn (1882–1974), a Polish immigrant, was one of the original partners in Metro-Goldwyn-Mayer, founded in 1925. He soon became an independent producer, developing major stars and authors.

William Randolph Hearst (1863–1951) was the son of California senator George Hearst and Phoebe Apperson Hearst, a noted philanthropist. William built a communications empire with a chain of newspapers, magazines, and radio stations. The classic movie *Citizen Kane* was based on Hearst's life.

Billie Jean King (1943–   ), a tennis star, was born in Long Beach. She held women's singles championships in England, the United States, Australia, Italy, and France. She is also well known for her efforts on behalf of women's tennis

Louis L'Amour (1908–1988) was known for his works of Western fiction. Born in North Dakota, he was a longtime resident of Los Angeles.

Billie Jean King

Dorothea Lange (1895–1965), a photographer, moved to San Francisco from the East Coast in 1918. Her most notable photos were of migrant workers during the Great Depression and of Japanese people held in U.S. relocation centers during World War II.

Jack London (1876–1916), born in San Francisco, was the author of *The Call of the Wild, White Fang,* and many other books and stories. He was one of the country's most widely read authors because of the action and adventure in his stories. His writings often explored the struggle for survival of characters with raw emotions.

Aimee Semple McPherson (1890–1944), an evangelist and faith healer, settled in Los Angeles in 1918 and founded the Four Square Gospel Church. She also broadcast her message on the radio. At the time of her death, her church had several hundred branches in the United States and Canada (her native land).

Marilyn Monroe (1926–1962), a Los Angeles–born actress, made more than fifteen movies during the 1950s, including *The Asphalt Jungle* and *Some Like It Hot.* She became a figure of glamour and style, and her death at the young age of thirty-six increased the public's fascination with her life. She is one of the most written-about stars of the twentieth century.

Julia Morgan (1872–1957), the first woman to graduate from the state university in mechanical engineering, went on to become an architect. Her first major work was the rebuilding of the Fairmont Hotel after the San Francisco earthquake and fire of 1906. Her most famous work, however, was the creation of William Randolph Hearst's estate at San Simeon.

Richard M. Nixon (1913–1994), thirty-seventh president of the United States, was born in Yorba Linda. Nixon served as a U.S. representative to Congress and as vice president during the Eisenhower administration. Running for president on the Republican ticket in 1960, he was narrowly defeated by John F. Kennedy. He ran again in 1968 and defeated Hubert H. Humphrey to become president. He was re-elected in 1972 but was forced to resign over the Watergate scandal in 1974. Nixon was the first U.S. president to travel to China. His term was also marked by controversy concerning the Vietnam War.

George S. Patton (1885–1945), born in San Gabriel, became known as Old Blood and Guts because of his daring and ruthlessness as a commander of U.S troops in Europe during World War II. He commanded Allied troops in North Africa and Europe during the war and was the commander of the Third Army, which crossed France and fought in the Battle of the Bulge in 1944. In 1945 he commanded U.S. occupation forces in Europe.

Linus Pauling (1901–1994) won a Nobel Prize in chemistry in 1954 for his discoveries about molecular structure and chemical bonds. He was awarded a Nobel Peace Prize in 1962 for his efforts to achieve a nuclear test ban. Although born in Oregon, he received his PhD from the California Institute of Technology and taught in California universities most of his life.

Ronald Reagan (1911–2004) was elected president of the United States in 1980 and served two terms, known as the Reagan years. Because of his abilities as a communicator and his personal style, he was a popular

Richard M. Nixon

president. Although born in Illinois, he traveled to California where he signed on as an actor with Warner Brothers. He also served as governor of California for eight years, elected in 1966 and 1970. During his presidency, he advocated conservative social and economic policies.

Malvina Reynolds (1901–1978) was a folksinger and social activist who opposed the Vietnam War. Born in San Francisco and a longtime resident of Berkeley, one of her most famous songs is "Little Boxes," a song about conformity and uniformity, which has been recorded by Joan Baez and others.

Sally Ride (1951–   ), born in Los Angeles, was the first American woman in space when she flew with a *Challenger* mission in 1983. In 1984 she returned to space aboard the same craft. She was part of the commission that investigated the explosion of the 1986 *Challenger* mission and is the author of *To Space and Back*.

Charles Schultz (1922–2000), born in Saint Paul, Minnesota, and a longtime resident of California, is well known to fans of Charlie Brown, Lucy, and Snoopy as the cartoonist behind the "Peanuts" comic strip. His cartoons are popular with both children and adults.

Isaac Stern (1920–2001), an outstanding violinist, was born in Russia but immigrated to San Francisco at age one. He made his debut with the San Francisco Symphony when he was eleven. He played and recorded with major orchestras around the world and helped the careers of many other important musicians. He also led the successful movement to save New York City's Carnegie Hall from demolition in 1960 and was influential in the creation of the National Endowment for the Arts in 1964.

Isaac Stern

Elizabeth Taylor (1932–   ) was born in England but became a state resident and a major Hollywood star as a child. At age twelve, she starred in *National Velvet.* As an adult, she starred in *Cleopatra* and *Who's Afraid of Virginia Woolf.* She is also known for her life of romance and wealth.

Shirley Temple (1928–   ) was a nationally known movie star by the time she was six years old. Born in Santa Monica, she was a talented actress, singer, and dancer. Temple starred in *Little Miss Marker, The Littlest Rebel, Rebecca of Sunnybrook Farm,* and many other movies during the 1930s. She received an honorary Academy Award in 1934. Retired from acting by 1950, she later served as U.S. representative to the General Assembly of the United Nations, U.S. ambassador to Ghana, and chief of protocol of the United States.

Earl Warren (1891–1974), born in Los Angeles, became chief justice of the United States Supreme Court in 1953. He had served three terms as governor of the state. As chief justice of the Supreme Court (1953–1969), he presided over a revolutionary period in the history of the Court. One of the Court's most important decisions during this period was to strike down school segregation as unconstitutional. In 1964 he headed a presidential commission to look into the assassination of President John F. Kennedy.

TOUR THE STATE

Lava Beds National Monument (Modoc and Siskiyou counties) This is a 46,560-square-acre preserve of chasms and caves formed by prehistoric volcanoes.

Columbia State Historic Park (Columbia) Twelve blocks of restored buildings re-create the town during gold-rush days. Buildings include a Wells Fargo office, a Masonic temple, saloons, stores, a firehouse, a schoolhouse, and a newspaper office.

Yosemite National Park (Tuolumne, Mariposa, and Madera counties) Visitors come to this national park to see spectacular natural attractions such as Bridalveil Falls, Yosemite Falls, Half Dome, El Capitan, Mirror Lake, and Yosemite Valley.

Sequoia and Kings Canyon national parks (Tulare County) Mount Whitney, the state's highest point, and the General Sherman giant redwood (275 feet) are located within Sequoia. Kings Canyon, just north of Sequoia, also features great groves of redwoods, including the General Grant tree (267 feet).

Death Valley National Park (Inyo County) This is one of the world's hottest and driest places. The area contains the country's lowest spot, Badwater, which is 282 feet below sea level. At its highest point, Telescope Peak, Death Valley is 11,049 feet above sea level. The area boasts a wealth of geological features: sand dunes, sculpted rocks, canyons, mountains, and volcanic craters.

Sea World (San Diego) This marine zoological park features killer whales, dolphins, sea lions, otters, and walruses. It also includes rides, aquariums, marine-life exhibits, a marina, and research labs.

Disneyland (Anaheim) This is a gigantic theme park in Anaheim. It was created by Walt Disney and features many "lands," including Fantasyland, Frontierland, Adventureland, Tomorrowland, Main Street U.S.A., Critter Country, and Mickey's Toontown.

Knott's Berry Farm (Buena Park) Founded as a roadside stand in 1920, today this is a large amusement park. It is divided into six areas representing different periods in the state's history.

Universal Studios Hollywood (Universal City) Take the *Back to the Future* ride here or a back-lot tour to see where some of your favorite movies were made. Watch demonstrations of special effects or see a television show or movie being filmed.

Mission San Juan Capistrano (Orange County) This is one of the twenty-one missions founded in California by the Spanish. Visitors tour the mission buildings and stop in the museum rooms covering the various periods of the mission's history, including the Native American, Spanish, and Mexican.

Monterey Bay Aquarium (Monterey) This is one of the largest aquariums in the world, with displays of more than five hundred species. It includes a two-story sea otter exhibit and a three-story kelp forest.

Winchester Mystery House (San Jose) This house has 160 rooms, two thousand doors, thirteen bathrooms, ten thousand windows, forty staircases, and many secret passageways. The owner, heiress to the Winchester fortune (rifles and guns), and her servants needed maps to find their way around. The heiress, a widow, began construction after consulting a seer who said that continuous building would appease the spirits of people killed with Winchester guns. Construction went on seven days a week for thirty-eight years.

Alcatraz Island (San Francisco Bay) Take a guided tour of a former maximum security federal prison. Al Capone, Machine Gun Kelly, and Robert Stroud (the Birdman of Alcatraz) were once jailed there.

Rim of the World Drive (San Bernardino County) This scenic drive winds for 40 miles with views of Lake Arrowhead, Big Bear Lake, and other panoramas.

Find Out More

Would you like to know more about California? Check the library, bookstore, or video store for these titles:

BOOKS

Altman, Linda Jacobs. *The Calforina Gold Rush in American History.* Springfield, NJ: Enslow, 1997.

Ansary, Mir Tamim. *California History.* Chicago: Heinemann, 2002.

Green, Carl R. *The Mission Trails in American History.* Springfield, NJ: 2000.

Keyworth, C. L. *California Indians.* New York: Facts on File, 1991.

Lee, Hector. *Heroes, Villains and Ghosts: Folklore of Old California.* Santa Barbara, CA: Capra Press, 1984.

————. *Tales of California.* Logan: Utah State University Press, 1974.

Savage, Jeff. *Gold Miners of the Wild West.* Springfield, NJ: Enslow, 1995.

Wills, Charles A. *A Historical Album of California.* Brookfield, CT: Millbrook Press, 1994.

VIDEOTAPES, MOVIES, AND TELEVISION

California's Gold. Narrated by Huell Howser. Sponsored by Wells Fargo Bank. (A series that aired on public broadcasting stations.)

The Frisco Kid. Warner Brothers, 1979. (A comedy about a rabbi from Poland who journeys to San Francisco in the 1860s.)

Last of His Tribe. Made-for-TV movie, 1992. (The story of Ishi, the Yahi Indian who walked into the mining town of Oroville, California, the last survivor of his people.)

ELECTRONIC MEDIA

America Alive. MediaAlive. CD-ROM, available in Macintosh and Windows versions. (Virtual tours include many places of interest in California: San Francisco, Magic Mountain Amusement Park, Death Valley, and others.)

The San Diego Zoo Presents . . . the Animals! Software Toolworks, Novato, CA. CD-ROM, available in Macintosh and Windows versions. (A virtual tour of the famous zoo.)

Story of the States. Parsippany, NJ: Bureau of Electronic Publishing. CD-ROM, available in Macintosh and Windows versions. (A multimedia trip to California and other states of the Union.)

WEB SITES

http://www.ca.gov
The state's official home page where you can find pictures, information, and suggestions for further research.

http://www.visitcalifornia.com/state/tourism/tour_homepage.jsp
This site leads you to things to do and places to see in the Golden State.

http://boxer.senate.gov/kids/index.cfm
This link takes you to the Kids Corner, part of the official Web site of U.S. Senator Barbara Boxer.

http://www.californiahistory.net/
A guide to the state's long and colorful history.

http://www.californiahistoricalsociety.org/programs/edu_materials.html
The Teachers and Students page of the California Historical Society Web site.

http://www.child.net/cakids.htm
A guide to resources, activities, and fun for children living across the state. Links lead to local areas and regions.

ABOUT THE AUTHOR

Linda Jacobs Altman lives with her husband, Richard, and their four cats, three dogs, and two cockatiels off a dirt road in the small town of Clearlake, California.

She has written many books for young readers, including a picture book about a migrant farmworker child, a history of migrant workers, and a biography of Cesar Chavez.

Index

Page numbers in boldface are illustrations and charts.